LYME DISEASE:

A MOTHER'S PERSPECTIVE

By

Karen Angotti

Mother of: Lisa Marie, David, and Jonathan

PUBLISHED BY
Anerak Publications
P.O. Box 1822
Cordova, TN 38018-1822

Copyright © 1993 by Karen Angotti
All Rights Reserved.
No part of this publication may be reproduced, stored in a retrieval system, or transmitted, in any form or by any means, electronic, mechanical, photocopying, recording, or otherwise, without the prior written permission of the copyright owner. Requests for permission or further information should be addressed to the publisher at the above address.

Some of the names in this book have been changed
to protect identities.

All Scripture quotations are from the King James Version.

Library of Congress Catalog Card Number: 92-73763

ISBN   0-9633902-3-6

Printed and bound in the United States of America.

Cover design by David Board

Dedicated to
Dr. Edwin J. Masters

A Doctor
Who truly deserves the title
Physician and **Healer**

A Doctor
Who with **Resourcefulness**
Found a disease in an unexpected place
And then
With **Compassion**
Endeavored to alleviate the suffering
And with **Courage**
Defend his position

From our family
Thank you

TABLE OF CONTENTS

Foreword / i

Chapter One--Our Family / 1

Chapter Two--**IT** Begins / 11

Chapter Three--The Mysterious Illness / 15

Chapter Four--Could It **Really** be Lyme? / 31

Chapter Five--A Reprieve / 35

Chapter Six--The Enemy Strikes Again / 37

Chapter Seven--The Hospital Again / 43

Chapter Eight--What Next? / 51

Chapter Nine--The Hospital Saga Continues / 59

Chapter Ten--One Day at a Time / 75

Epilogue / 81

Facts About Lyme Disease / 87

Suggestions for Better Medical Care / 91

Lyme Newsletters / 96

If I can stop one Heart from breaking
I shall not live in vain
If I can ease one Life the Aching
Or cool one Pain
Or help one fainting Robin
Unto his Nest again
I shall not live in Vain

Emily Dickenson

I am only one person, but I am one.
I cannot do everything, but I can do something.
And what I can do, by the grace of God, I will do.

Helen Keller

A man who knows that the earth is round but lives among men who believe it to be flat ought to hammer in his doctrine of the earth's roundness up to the point of arrest, imprisonment, or even death. Reality will confirm him and he is not so much testifying to the world as it is--which is worth nothing--as to Him who made the world, and Who is worth more than all things.

Hilaire Belloc

FOREWORD

When my son David was around five and had been experiencing a series of puzzling, week-long 105 degree temperatures, he commented, "Mom, you always love us, but when we are sick, you **REALLY** love us." Nothing could explain how much a mother loves her children. The children themselves cannot begin to fathom the depth of this love; and oftentimes we say, "When you have children of your own, you will understand." As I read back over what I have written, I realize that I cannot hope to convey the absolute terror that I felt as I watched my straight, healthy son drop to a crumpled, pitiful mass of humanity. My fear of his death or permanent disability was extreme. With no diagnosis, the doctors' assurances that he was not dying in no way reassured me. I struggled desperately to hide my extreme fear because the doctors were already convinced that I was overly concerned and anxious. Believing that I was a fairly logical, intelligent person, it had never occurred to me that there was a disease so baffling that it could totally stymie the medical profession and that it could thwart any of my feeble attempts to explain its symptoms rationally. It also had never occurred to me that I might suddenly be thrust in the midst of a medical controversy, a war waged between intellectuals far removed from the actual bloody battlefields of the disease itself. If the generals want to know if the enemy has invaded a territory, the best place to gain information is from the foot soldiers and scouts already there in position and taking hits. And care and treatment of the wounded should not be dictated by far removed, untouched higher ups but by experienced, combat field marshalls on the frontlines who are in a position to judge the efficacy of their efforts. Further, the war should not be classififed Top Secret with no field reports leaked for fear of alarming the public. After all, this battle is being waged on the homefront. Women and children, mothers and babies, young and old, all are at risk.

My purpose in writing this book is fourfold. One, I hope to educate, inform, and prevent you, the reader, from having your own story to tell. Though some people are aware of the disease and its major vector, ticks. Most are unaware of the serious ramifications of the illness and the difficulty of diagnosing and treating it. <u>It is not an easily cured infection</u>. Researchers have cultured the bacteria from patients who have supposedly received adequate I.V. therapy.[1] Even with early diagnosis and treatment, some people progress on to the later stages of central nervous system involvement. Some may never be cured and some will actually die. Though I found ticks distasteful, repulsive, pesky critters, I was not afraid of them at all. My main concern for my children was to avoid the snakes in the woods. Though the tick's "poison" is much slower acting than that of a rattlesnake, it can be deadly and life changing. The person who lived in our house before us died of ALS. When she moved in, she was perfectly healthy. Two years later she was diagnosed with ALS and two years after that she dies. ALS is one of the diseases that can be confused with Lyme disease. No one will ever know if she had Lyme, but I will always wonder. Some estimates purport that seven to ten percent of ALS victims may in actuality be Lyme victims. Is it possible that more people are dying from this illness than is realized? Without a healthy amount of fear, this disease is not going to be prevented. If people continue blithely on their way unconcerned about the ticks, this disease will continue to spread. Prevention, as with any disease, is the best course.

Secondly, I hope to share with other Lyme victims our story and perhaps with the realization that they are not alone help in some small way. The feeling that you are the only person in the world experiencing rejection, humiliation, and disbelief is incapcitating and crippling. Uniting with fellow sufferers via support groups and newsletters can empower us with enough strength to go on and to fight the prejudices that presently exist. There is strength in numbers. As our numbers swell, it will be more and more difficult to doubt our veracity and particularly troublesome, our sanity.

1. Preac-Mursic, Weber, et al. Survival of *Borrelia burgdorferi* in antibiotically treated patients with Lyme Borreliosis. 1989, Infection 17 No. 5. Six cases were cultured <u>after</u> what was thought to be appropriate antibiotic therapy.

FOREWORD

Thirdly, with an awareness of the serious nature of this disease and its potential threat to everyone who at any time may encounter a tick bite (or, according to some scientific studies, a mosquito, flea, or biting fly bite), I hope to press for legislation for more research and education. Without public outcry and concern, our hard earned tax dollars will be spent on perhaps some less worthy endeavor. Contacting your senators and representatives is as easy as picking up your phone or writing a letter. Both have a big impact. Our representatives cannot represent us properly without our input. They will not know that their constituents are being plagued with this illness if they are not informed. Your story is vital.

Finally, to the small number of medical professionals who may possibly read this narrative, I would like to plead with you to give your patients the benefit of the doubt. I am sure that in your day to day encounters with numerous patients that there may be a few who are truly hypochondriacs who waste your time and rile your nerves. But, on the offside chance that this particular person has a legitimate complaint and medicine has just not elevated to the point of determining this readily, why not think long and hard before labeling him with a hard-to-shake description. Keep an open mind, instead of eliminating the easiest most probable diagnosis and then immediately turning to psychology for an answer. We are helpless in your hands. We need you. Because of our great need of you, you have earned a position of respect and honor that is almost impossible to match in our society. To save a life or return someone's health, could there be anything more rewarding or fulfilling? Could there be anything more frightening than to neglect someone's complaint and watch them die or deteriorate? Your responsibility is so awesome and I would not want to be in your shoes. No one expects you to be perfect. No one expects you never to make a mistake. However, we do expect you to _listen._ Listen carefully, with your heart as well as your mind. Though we may seem like a mass of sore throats, ear aches, swollen joints, and various and sundry body parts and complaints, we are not. We are human beings. With imperfections and faults much like your own, we are part of the teeming mass of humanity. When we come to you for care, we place in your hands a unique and irreplaceable person. Someone who loves and is loved. Someone who can be hurt by your words as well as your deeds. Maybe when someone is being particularly irritating, you can stop and remember that this person is probably sick, hurting, and scared. And maybe when what someone is saying does not make sense, you can remember that there is much yet to be learned about the human body and medicine and that no one will fault you for saying, "I don't know." And if you say, "I don't know, but I'll try to help you," you probably will have that person's undying gratitude and lifelong devotion. We need you. May God help you as you meet this need.

An article in *The New York Times* entitled "How Tools of Medicine Can Get in the Way" illustrates vividly how doctors can become so enamored "with medical technology that they forget one of the cardinal rules of medicine --**listening** to the patient and learning by using their hands and stethoscopes in the traditional physical examination." Dr. Yee, a surgeon from California, had a fever of 101, nausea, and severe abdominal pain. After experiencing an EKG, numerous blood tests that did not show an elevated white blood cell count, X-rays for kidney stones, a CT scan, and a three day delay, he was found to have a ruptured appendix. He had been convinced he had appendicitis for two days before the doctors were persuaded to operate; and, even then, the operation was performed for another condition, not appendicitis. The hospital cost was probably $20,000 more than if the operation had been done on admission to the hospital; and, instead of two weeks of recuperation, he lost five weeks away from the office. Appendicitis is a condition that is diagnosed almost exclusively from a medical history and physical examination. Quoting the article, "No test or technology has improved the diagnosis except by identifying other causes of abdominal pain. But surgeons are not expected to wait until tests rule out every other condition before they operate." Technology has its place. Technology has its usefulness, but there are diseases that cannot be readily diagnosed even with all the modern technology we have available today. Lyme disease is one condition in which it is crucial that the doctor simply listens to the patient. To continue to quote the article, ". . . diseases do not always appear in classic form and . . . the variations can fool the best doctors."

Medical science has made such rapid advancements in the past century that often it is regarded with such awe that the ordinary person feels that he cannot begin to understand any of it. Most of us know that George Washington was bled to death by the best doctors our country had to offer and that this practice was so engrained that doctors continued it

FOREWORD

long after it was proven to kill. A few know of Louis Pasteur's twenty-five year struggle to have the medical community accept his work on immunizations and germs and how Semmelweis was hounded to an early death after his observation that washing hands between the morgue and delivery of a baby would save lives. Yet, these events are considered so far in the past as to have little impact on today's medical "science." Looking closely at the near past though, one finds that there are examples of failures even closer at hand. The DES tragedy is one that is affecting thousands and the scope of its ramifications is still not fully known. When AIDS was first being observed, it was termed a "genetic" illness of homosexuals. How many people did this erroneous conclusion kill? Only a few years ago, people with acne were treated with irradiation until it was discovered that they were then developing thymus cancer. Daily, people are sent home with a diagnosis of indigestion to die of heart attacks and cancer. Procedures and operations that are today the rage can easily be discarded in a few years. Medicine, with its regal trappings and lofty ideals, is still not perfect. And we, doctors and patients alike, had best remember it.

Once on Long Island, a man purchased an expensive barometer. Carefully, assembling it, he became extremely disgusted and irate as he could not force it to work. It was registering no pressure whatsoever. Dashing off an angry letter to the manufacturer, he stuffed it back in its box and left the Island to go to work. When he returned, not only was the barometer gone, but so was his house and everything in it. A huge hurricane had completely destroyed much of the Island. The barometer had not been wrong. The interpretation was wrong. The man's preconceived impression that the barometer should be registering prevented him from recognizing a real and present danger. Throughout life, we must guard against allowing our preconceived notions from coloring the facts of a situation. At times, it is a matter of life and death.

LITTLE PEOPLE

A dreary place would be this earth
Were there no little people in it;
The Song of life would lose its mirth,
Were there no children to begin it.

No little forms, like buds to grow,
And make the admiring heart surrender
No little hands on breast and brow,
To Keep the thrilling love-chords tender.

The sterner souls would grow more stern,
Unfeeling nature more inhuman,
And man to stoic coldness turn,
And Woman would be less than woman.

Life's song, indeed, would lose its charm,
Were there no babies to begin it;
A doleful place this world would be,
Were there no little people in it.

-----*John Greenleaf Whittier*

Lo, children are a heritage of the Lord: and the fruit of the womb is his reward. As arrows are in the hand of a mighty man; so are children of the youth. Happy is the man that hath his quiver full of them: they shall not be ashamed, but they shall speak with the enemies in the gate.

Psalms 127:3-5 KJV

CHAPTER ONE

Our Family

Vivid, verdant greens brush breathtakingly across an azure blue sky. My eyes feast on the array of color displayed outside my kitchen window, and I smile in contentment as I contemplate living in this idyllic beauty the rest of my life. My gaze shifts downward to the clamor of young voices at the base of the trees. Faces flushed and gleaming, three blonde-haired, blue-eyed munchkins are spinning and twirling on a rope swing hanging from the trees. My pride, my joy, in fact, I believe the major reason for God placing me on this earth--my children. The untrained observer would not realize that the green canopy had become a Big Top or recognize that the young man had transformed into a ringmaster bellowing out the amazing feats of the two garishly attired acrobats pirouetting at the end of the rope. They love our new home. Even though we have only been here a couple of weeks, they seem to have settled in with barely a ripple, exploring the forest with a relish; capturing frogs, turtles, and insects; fishing in the pond; and searching furiously for Civil War bullets and treasure. In their minds, every square foot of the South must be covered with relics and artifacts. Every new experience is greeted with a wonder found only in children. Living in a city neighborhood in San Jose, California, for the past twelve years, they had only dreamed of the freedom and experiences that they could now enjoy on a daily basis. Frank, my husband, and I also are experiencing an exhilarating sense of freedom. No longer do the baseballs fly over a fence into the neighbor's yard never to be seen again. No longer do we glance fearfully down the street looking for cars as the kids scream down the driveway on their bikes. And no longer do I find myself wondering about kidnapping attempts. There had been two the previous summer in our old neighborhood. We feel truly blessed.

Lisa Marie, our twelve-year-old, is a typical oldest child, very conscientious and responsible. A woman-child, one moment she is playing dolls or cavorting in childhood games with her brothers; and, the next, she is a sophisticated teenager with all the answers to the universe. She has always had a maturity beyond her years and a desire to please making her very appealing to adults. At the age of two and a half, she could say the alphabet, count, quote memory verses, recite nursery rhymes, say all the books of the Bible in order, and sing numerous songs.

We delighted in watching her grow and learn, laughing when people would think she learned these things from *Sesame Street*, which she never watched. By age four, she could read and started school soon thereafter. School was a joy for her and everything seemed easy. In fact, so easy I wondered why they did not have more assignments. When the boys came along, I discovered why they did not have more. Sitting still in the classroom, following orders, and doing her work almost perfectly won her many awards as "Student of the Day", "Student of the Week", and "Student of the Month." Such a contrast from the boys; she enjoyed frilly dresses and a CLEAN room. As she grew, she learned to cook and to clean and began to help with the household chores. Jonathan was born when she was almost seven and she immediately became a second little mother, eventually changing diapers and making herself indispensable to her brother. By age twelve, she was already beginning to be in demand as a responsible, caring baby sitter, but her full schedule left little time for it. She began playing the piano for the Junior High youth group on Sundays and was becoming quite a little gymnast, performing aerials and back flips with no hands. The sport became her favorite activity surpassing soccer at which she was also becoming quite competent. She earned the nick-name "Bigfoot" on her team for her powerful, field-long kicks. Boys are beginning to enter the picture, but we (Mom and Dad) are doing our best to ignore them. In fact, one mother told me she had already picked Lisa to marry her son. Our sweet, little angel is becoming quite the little lady.

David. Energetic. Enthusiastic. Creative. Imaginative. Irrepressible. Impetuous. Outgoing. Optimistic. Persistent. Inquisitive. The adjectives to describe our extroverted ten-year-old seem endless. From the time he could roll over, changing his diaper became a challenge of wits, speed, and endurance. The child was never still. He earned the nickname "Hurricane

Dave" from his uncle by the age of two. Wherever David is, excitement follows. He played with older children oftentimes, and he was always the instigator of one adventure after another. He began building roller coasters at the age of five. With the aid of skate boards, gravity, and a push, he could manage a quite exciting ride on his homemade contraptions. He was never happier than when he was creating. One of the worst punishments we could administer was to take away his wood building privileges for a time.

Despite the flurry of activity on the outside, he possesses a very tender heart that sometimes others miss. At the age of five, we saw a stretcher being loaded into an ambulance. David became convinced that the person was dead and became very upset. Trying to comfort him, I remarked, "Well, we really didn't know the person anyway." He protested, "Well, we would have liked them if we did." And indeed he would have. His attitude toward everyone big and little alike is to treat them as a friend. A people person like his father, the word stranger does not seem to be in his vocabulary. He talks constantly to anyone who will listen and tends to keep them in stitches with his sometimes quite startling comments.

It soon became apparent that he had a logical, analytical mind. When he was eight, he became very interested in baseball and asked his father the distance between the bases. Frank replied, "It's exactly ninety feet." Quickly David uttered, "Wow, that's 360 feet all the way around." Realizing that he did not know his multiplication tables, I was startled and queried, " How did you do that problem?" He said, "Well, ninety is almost a hundred; that makes four hundred; then subtract 40. Easy Mom." Frank and I glanced at each other and quickly determined that this child better not ever bring home a low grade in math! He loves to read but the books have to be adventures and mysteries or filled with experiments, tricks, or jokes. He enjoys most sports, but baseball has become the without a doubt favorite and the Oakland A's his most favorite team. He declares that one day he intends to be a professional baseball player. The rest of the family often enjoys speculating on just what career our little livewire will pursue.

Jonathan, our five-year-old, is the baby, but most of the time it is hard to think of him in that role. He has spent his entire life trying not to be a baby and attempting to do everything that his older brother does. And when I say everything, I mean everything. As a two-year-old, waitresses would look at us very strangely when we told them, "Thank you, but, no, we do not need a booster seat or highchair." To this day when we go to a restaurant to order a meal, he orders exactly what David does and if David changes his order (which he does just for this reaction) so does Jonathan. In our house, baby teeth are primary teeth; and Christmas presents have to be purchased very carefully to ensure that Jonathan does not think that David's gifts are better than his. We did manage to buy David a chemistry set without upsetting Jonathan too much. Between his persistence and his coordination, he is a very good athlete. He learned to ride a bicycle at the age of three and currently despises T ball because he thinks that it is too easy (babyish) after playing ball so much with his brother. He has a passion for bugs and his one requirement for moving to Tennessee was that the place have lots and lots of insects. He got his wish and then some. One has to be very careful opening containers around our house or you may find yourself face to face with a winged, multi-legged critter ready to attack. Since our move, fishing and exploring have become favorite pastimes. Our country home is a little boy's dream with turtles, frogs, toads, and wildlife in abundance. The two boys wish for the day that they can hunt the deer, opossum, rabbits, and squirrels that abound. Actually I am very proud of my two all boy boys, but there are days that I wish for a little less dirt, noise, and excitement.

Frank is everything a woman could want in a husband. When we first met in college, I was skeptical that he could truly possess all the good qualities that appeared on the surface, but the more I learned the more I found that he was everything he seemed and more. He is kind and considerate, always conferring with me on any major and most minor decisions that affect our lives. If all men had as much respect for women as Frank, women's liberation would have been unnecessary and nonexistent. After sixteen years of marriage I am still amazed that God blessed me by allowing me to marry such an honest, upright man.

In high school, he was the starting center for the basketball team, and basketball is still one of his favorite recreational activities. Between sports, church activities, and part time jobs, he had very little free time. He was president of the church youth group and played his guitar and sang in groups and solos. As a paper boy, he earned trips to Florida, New York City, and Washington D.C. These were earned by selling newspaper subscriptions in his hometown which was thirty-five miles from Cleveland where the paper was printed, and no one from his city had ever won anything before. It was said that it couldn't be done. After graduation, he was recommended by his guidance counselor to a family with a handicapped son who needed an attendant in college. In exchange for his tuition, Frank cared for this boy's personal needs. The next year the boy's brother was able to provide this service, so Frank with no funds to continue his education in the height of the Viet Nam era joined the Army. This was the only branch of the military which would accept you into a flight program without a college degree, and flying was his dream.

While serving as a helicopter pilot in Viet Nam, he was shot down and burned on over twenty percent of his body. He almost died and most of his crew did die. In the hospital recovering from his injuries, he felt guilty for living wondering why he lived and the others died. Finally, he determined that God wanted him alive for some specific reason and that he would not question God's plan. He came back from Viet Nam well aware of how short life is and resolved to make his life count. This stint in the Army earned him a Purple Heart, two Bronze Stars, twenty-six Air Medals, and a coveted unit safety award. (In Viet Nam, the other soldiers always wanted to fly with Frank because his cautious reputation made them feel that he would bring them home safe.) Determining that he wanted to be an airline pilot, he then plotted the course. Doggedly following it despite negative input from college professors and other pilots who thought it an impossible dream. In 1978, just before our first baby was born, he achieved his goal. He was hired by Flying Tigers since purchased by Federal Express. The interviewer told him that he had been selected out of a file of 20,000 applicants. Practically all the new hires were from California where the company was based and most had a contact within the company. Believing God to be in control of every aspect of our lives, we did not think that it was chance that Frank was one of the few to be chosen from out of state and with no inside recommendations whatsoever. Within a few months, he was flying a 747, the largest commercial aircraft, exceeding his wildest expectations. Recently while upgrading to captain, the FAA inspector complimented him on his crew management, adding, "But then that comes naturally to you." He does have strong leadership capabilities and has always been able to lead without being dictatorial, overbearing, or obnoxious; his strong, calm, easygoing manner putting people at ease.

Our lives revolved around our church, and soon Frank became at various times a deacon, adult Sunday School teacher, head usher, and chairman of the mission's committee. I was just as involved for my part, teaching Sunday School and playing the piano for the choir.

As a father, he put much time and preparation into doing it right. My memories of him playing with our children are some of my most precious. I can see him sitting in the floor while little Lisa feeds him some imaginary concoction which he immediately tosses in the air announcing that it is too hot while the two kids explode with laughter, giving wheelbarrow rides in the midst of planting trees in the backyard, building teetering towers of blocks and Legos, cycling with a small person strapped in a child carrier, patiently pushing a bicycle until the little one suddenly acquired the knack of staying upright, tossing endless balls and hitting numerous flies, taking the boys to ball games and once Lisa to the ballet, playing roll-around (our version of rough housing), singing them their especially composed-just-for-them songs at bedtime, and, in general, just enjoying and loving our children.

As a child, I learned firsthand how teasing, taunts, and rejection made one feel. I never called the shortest boy in the class, Runt, or the kid with the long neck whose mother shaved his head in the dead of winter, Super Turtle. Though they became known almost exclusively by these nicknames, I could not bear to cause them pain. Similarly, I never teased the boy who suffered from epilepsy or the two retarded children in our class. One of the greatest pains I could suffer would be to feel that I had hurt someone. Once a very poor boy in my class (his home did not even have windows and he often did not have shoes) came to school with an Easter basket filled with real grass instead of the plastic, artificial kind. Immediately, the cruel laughter and jesting began. Unable to bear it, I told the joksters to stop. This resulted in their taunts being turned on me for months, but to this day defending that child, small deed that it was, is something that I am proud of. I wish oftentimes that I could be like Frank ignoring insults and letting them slide off his back, but somehow I seem to take them to heart and allow them to hurt me all the more.

In high school, I was extremely active in 4-H winning several county and state events and some out of state trips. Musically, I was involved in competition in both voice and piano, making a trip to New York City to play the piano. I graduated valedictorian of my high school class and fourth in the standings in my college class. Science, math, anything with logical conclusions came easily to me. Though I could not understand why such things should matter to boys, if it did not matter to me, it seemed to. One boy I met in college began regaling me with his ACT science and math scores. Realizing where this was leading, I tried desperately to change the subject, but, sure enough, he asked about mine. End of budding romance. Fortunately, Frank is not intimidated by such things and is confident enough in his own abilities to respect me for mine. After fourteen years as a housewife, these things have almost passed into oblivion. They are virtually never a topic in any conversation, and my friends since that time are unaware of this part of my past. But as I spent over half of my life attaining these goals, I suppose that they are an important part of who I am.

Actually, I am not terribly impressed by such things as grades, titles, power, or money. Throughout our courtship, Frank was terribly frustrated trying to impress me. He took me to see the helicopters he flew in Viet Nam. My response, "They look just like the toy ones." (He says that that comment almost stopped him from asking me out again.) It took him a long time to realize that I could be impressed but usually only by character traits such as kindness, compassion, honesty, and humility. When these are combined with traits that are customarily honored then it tips the scale, and I bestow on that person my greatest respect. Obtaining someone's autograph or shaking hands with famous people has never been one of my goals either. I much prefer an intimate conversation with one or two people really learning what makes that person tick or even reading a biography to a superficial greeting in person.

When my grandmother was told of the arrival of my first baby, she chuckled, "Well, now Karen finally has a baby to hold." At every family gathering, I had begged for this privilege. I knew I would love my baby, but no one could have explained how fiercely and protectively. Nor could they have told me how all other babies would suddenly pale in comparison. The responsibility of raising this solemn-eyed, little creature to competent adulthood was awesome. My response to this unknown was quite predictable considering the amount of time I had spent in libraries over my lifetime. I started reading books on child training. Over the years I would imagine I have read at least a couple hundred, picking and choosing the ideas that I believed would incorporate into our family.

Sharing my love of reading with the children became one of my great joys. I started reading to them before they could walk or talk, and by the time Lisa was six or so, we were reading the longer children's classics. We have laughed together over the antics of *Anne of Green Gables*, *Tom Sawyer*, and *Huckleberry Finn*; cried over the animals in *Bambi*, *Where the Red Fern Grows*, and *White Fang*; been held in suspense by books such as *The House of Sixty Fathers*, *The Witch at Blackbird Pond*, and *Carry On, Mr. Bowditch*; and puzzled over man's inhumanity to man in biographies such as *If I Perish* and *Tortured for the Faith*.

I consider myself a professional mother. Professional in the sense that I have spent years in on the job training and studying for this position. I took my vitamins and avoided all medications while I was pregnant. I breast fed, blended homemade baby food, and used cloth diapers. I stayed up at night through fevers and colic. I decorated birthday cakes and sewed outfits for special occasions. I made curtains, put up wallpaper, and stenciled their rooms. I dispensed large helpings of discipline covered completely by layers and layers of love. This was not some supreme sacrifice. After all, we could have afforded formula, baby food, and Pampers. I did all these things because I wanted to. Nothing on earth can quite compare to the joy one feels with a small babe nestled to one's breast. Moments before the picture of abject misery, after satisfying his initial hunger, he forgets about the warm milk for a moment and smiles the most beautiful, toothless smile. The joy that that smile brings is as difficult to describe as explaining the beauty of a sunset to a blind man or the thrill of a symphony to the deaf. That smile makes all the sleepless nights, the dirty diapers, and other myriad inconveniences worth it.

Of course, motherhood has its downside, too. Once when Frank was out of town (He seems to manage to be out of town for a lot of unanticipated crises including the birth of one baby.), Jonathan pours a whole bottle of glue down the toilet. Now this would not have been a problem except that underneath the opaque whiteness resting innocently on the bottom of the bowl was also the glue bottle. The children use and flush the toilet resulting in copious amounts of water and excrement gushing out onto the bathroom floor. Rushing in, I pull towels off the racks and begin mopping up the filthy mess. I try the plunger but succeed in only splashing more mess on me and the floor. Sternly, sending Jonathan to his room, I go downstairs to calm down and console myself. With eyes closed, I lean back on the sofa. With horror, I hear the unmistakable sound of splattering, splashing water streaming out of the kitchen cabinets onto the countertops and floor. Grabbing more towels, I furiously begin soaking up the germy water. All the dishes will have to be disinfected and cleaned, and the cabinets will have to be completely emptied, cleaned, and repapered. By the time the plumbers have unseated the toilet, poured even more aromatic ooze throughout the bathroom, and tramped the mess throughout the house, Timbuctoo begins to seem more appealing by the moment, not for me, of course, but for Jonathan. Perhaps, they do not have indoor plumbing. Occasionally, as I pass his room with a load of towels, he timidly questions whether he can come out. Each time, I reply, "No, not yet." This will most likely always be my most memorable Mother's Day. Frank calls from Hong Kong to wish me a quick Happy Mother's Day and ends up hearing a blow by blow description of the preceding events. He says that it will always be the most expensive Mother's Day ever after paying for the plumbers and the overseas long distance charges. Two weeks later, Jonathan flushes the dog tags.

Despite the ups and downs of parenting, Frank and I cherish our children. They are our link with the future; perhaps our most important way of impacting humanity. Their behavior and personalities have been scrutinized carefully by both of us. To us, these small humans are not toys or pets, but rather young saplings to be nourished, protected, and trained until they can take their own place in the forest. We periodically discuss which one may need more individualized attention, more discipline, more time reading, more time exercising, different friends, more sleep, more chores. Are we expecting too much from them at this time? Too little? Raising our children is our primary responsibility, more important than any other outside job or activity.

I suppose we are somewhat idealistic. We believe that "to whom much is given, much shall be required," and that we are some of the ones to whom God has given much, not in terms of material possessions but in terms of His unfailing love, mercy, and grace. We believe in setting goals, even unreachable goals, believing it is much better to have tried and failed than never to have tried at all. If we had not worked hard at parenting, then we would not have had the measure of success with our family that we have had. Oh, we know that we are far from perfect parents. We have failed many times, but we pick ourselves up and say, "OK, that's the way not to do it." Our goal is not an impossible-to-obtain perfection, but rather an attainable-with-work excellence. We know that our children have flaws; in fact, we can see their flaws and imperfections more clearly than anyone. But, as the saying goes, "God isn't finished with me yet." and neither are we finished shaping and molding our children. It would not surprise me to one day see one of my children in a position in the White House, overseas as a missionary, or at home in any number of jobs. But, wherever they are I expect them to be hardworking, patriotic, productive, caring, God-fearing individuals who realize how blessed they have been and who desire to help their fellowman.

This is our family and this is our story.

CHAPTER TWO

IT BEGINS
AUGUST 24, 1990

Midmorning, David comes in clutching his stomach insisting that he must see a doctor immediately. All three children have had a virus the past three or four days, with the typical upset stomachs, headaches, and fever. So, mildly exasperated, I admonish, "David, you know that a doctor can't do anything for a virus. You shouldn't have eaten that yogurt this morning. You know milk products make stomach aches worse."

"But Mom," he persists, "this feels much worse than a virus. And if it is milk products, then I am NEVER eating them again." Telling him to lie down, I note that he does look extremely pale. As he continues to complain vocally, I reluctantly determine that I am going to be forced to find a doctor. We have lived in Tennessee less than a month; I do not know the status of our insurance, have the slightest idea which doctor to use, or know my way around the city. Resignedly, I start making phone calls.

Sitting in the doctor's office later that afternoon, I feel very uncomfortable; knowing that if this is nothing more than a virus, we will be starting off on the wrong foot with this particular doctor. David looks awful, and, surprisingly, the doctor seems very concerned after finding that his temperature is 103 and his white blood cell count is abnormally elevated. Diagnosis, probable appendicitis. Quickly, arrangements are made to admit him to the hospital. My anxiety level is not terribly high until the doctor tells me that he believes that the appendix has already ruptured. My grandfather died from a ruptured appendix; and realizing the complications that could result, I swiftly drive the twenty minute, unfamiliar journey to the children's hospital praying that I do not get lost and lose precious time.

Relieved to arrive at the hospital, I still feel very alone knowing that Frank is out of town and that I will perhaps be making life and death decisions by myself. After his examination, the surgeon feels there is a sixty percent chance that David has appendicitis given the history of the other ill family members. The percentage would be higher without this factor, but the risk is too great to delay surgery. Fearing this is all unnecessary, I somewhat reluctantly consent to the surgery agreeing with the surgeon that the risk is too great.

After an anxious hour calling relatives and making arrangements for the other children, the surgeon informs me that the operation was a success. The appendix was indeed inflamed, and though not actually ruptured there is a strong possibility of pinhole-sized leaks as there was some pus in the abdomen. From his explanation and continued concern, I ascertain that this could potentially cause as many problems as if the appendix had actually ruptured.

Happily, David improves rapidly, and the biopsy of the appendix shows no leaks. Within a couple of days, he is joking incessantly with the nurses and traversing the halls as quickly as his IV pole will allow. The hospital seems to be too small for this active, easily bored ten year old, and I am relieved when we receive the good news of our release. As we sign the discharge papers, a nurse comments, "He seems to be a very nice, little boy." I reply, "Thank you. Of course, he is very special to us." Another nurse glances up at this and queries, "Is he your only one?" Puzzled, I shake my head surmising that not everyone cherishes their children the way we do. With light hearts, we leave the hospital very grateful that the necessity for being there had not been more serious and believing that it will be a long, long time before we have to enter its halls again.

This was not to be.

David, My Brother

David, my brother, is a typical boy,
So, I suspect you know that he likes to annoy.
David, my brother, is never shy.
Sometimes, so much I think I'll die.
David, my brother, has a dream,
To play one day on a professional baseball team.
David, my brother, is a whiz at math;
But, English is where he deposits his wrath.
David, my brother, is becoming courteous and kind.
He opens doors for Mom and me and doesn't seem to mind.
David, my brother, though he likes to think so, is not a sage,
For he is only ten short years of age.
Right now, I know that I'm bigger and stronger;
But, soon my "little" brother will be little no longer.

Lisa Marie Angotti
Age: 12

DAVID'S SONG

David Lee was a good, little boy,
And a good, little boy was he.
Oh, he climbed up in a tree one day,
    To see what he could see,
    To see what he could see.

Well, he looked to the north,
  And he looked to the south, to the east and west.
He looked all over the whole, wide world,
    To see which was best,
    To see which was best.

Before he knew what had happened,
David slipped and fell.
And as he lay upon the ground, he said,
    "All is not well."
    "All is not well."

He broke his hand and he broke his nose.
He broke his elbow, too.
He broke his knee, and he broke his big toe.
    He was all black and blue.
    He was all black and blue.

Now, David Lee is a good, little boy,
A good, little boy is he.
And when he climbs up in a tree,
    He's as careful as can be.
    He's as careful as can be.

                ----Love, Dad
                        1982

A wise son maketh a glad father.
                    Proverbs 15:20a

CHAPTER THREE

THE MYSTERIOUS ILLNESS
TWO WEEKS LATER

David is having terrible chest pains, an excruciating headache with dizziness and what we come to call falling episodes. During these perhaps thirty second intervals, he will clutch me with whitened knuckles, close his eyes, and beg me not to let him fall. As we are rushing him to the hospital, my mind is searching for anything that could explain his strange symptoms. He had complained of a couple of chest pains in the past week which I had dismissed as unimportant in his presence, but which I had intended to mention to the surgeon at his two week checkup especially as the doctors had asked me about his supposedly innocent heart murmur just before surgery. It had been considered so minor as a baby that it had almost completely slipped my mind until they brought it up. He had been so tired since the surgery, seemingly abnormally so. Having had three C-sections myself, I had expected him to recuperate at least as quickly as I had, if not faster. Last night, we took him out to his favorite restaurant to perk him up and then stopped by a department store for a few minutes. He looked so pale and wan that I berated myself for causing him to overdo, and even more so when he began saying his legs felt like jelly. Today, he looks every bit as bad as he did the day of the appendectomy. All I want to do is to get to the hospital and for someone to tell me what is wrong.

After many tests and much consulting, the doctors seem convinced that David is having a reaction to the anesthesia used during surgery. The slightly elevated liver enzymes seem to bear out this theory, and they have decided to admit him to the hospital to monitor his condition. Reassured that this could indeed cause all of his symptoms and that it is treatable, I relax, glad to be in such competent hands.

Thirty hours in this place and still no one has checked the records to see if David was actually given the particular anesthesia that causes the liver problems. The doctors do not seem to think that this is the answer as his liver enzymes have not risen any higher, but just to be on the safe side they are calling in a well respected internist, Dr. Hardman[1]. Efficiently determining that David was not given the implicated anesthetic, Dr. Hardman performs an endoscopy revealing a mild gastritis, but nothing else. More and more we are hearing about the innocuous virus, and comments are being made like, "Don't let him get too attached to his bed." or "Don't make an invalid of him." The incongruity of these remarks would be humorous, if the situation did not seem so serious. A fish out of water would be more comfortable than David would be staying in bed all the time. We are still very concerned, but the doctors are not. They tell us that he is not dying. We are not reassured, unable to understand how they can be so adamant without a diagnosis. Though they do not come right out and say they want us to leave the hospital, one doctor says something about our insurance not paying. This is infuriating, and we assume a threat. First of all, we did not ask to have him admitted. This decision was made by several doctors in emergency and evidently was a bungled diagnosis. Secondly, we had never asked for him to remain there; we had just been uneasy with their conclusions and very inquisitive. This yielded several differences of opinion. One would say the elevated sedimentation rate could be caused by a virus, another would disagree. One would say to make him walk, another would say not to make a person with ataxia walk. We leave the hospital, disappointed and disheartened, with one very, very sick little boy.

During this visit, the surgeon, whom I respect tremendously as he truly cared about my son, came to examine David. He is the first and only doctor in Tennessee to ask about a tick bite. We had recently read an article on Lyme disease brought over by a neighbor, and we reply, "Yes, he was bitten several times, but he did not have a rash. " This ends the discussion, and we do not consider this possibility again for some time.

At home, David's symptoms seem only to worsen. The dizziness is increasing, and he does not want to walk to the bathroom or even raise his

---

[1] This is a fictitious name.

THE MYSTERIOUS ILLNESS 17

head off the pillow because of the "nails" in his head. He says that if he is lying down, the nails only stick in about an inch or so, but if he sits up, they push halfway in. And if he stands, they ram all the way into his head. The chest pains scare us badly, but we struggle to conceal this from David. We see an ear, nose, and throat specialist to determine if an inner ear problem could be causing the dizziness. Then a pediatric neurologist who orders a CAT scan which is normal. The neurologist's opinion is possible migraines. He uses the word possible because one does not diagnose migraines on the basis of one headache. Though we have never heard of week long migraines, he assures us that there is such a thing, though rare. Still not convinced, I ask if migraines cause chest pain noting that these began at the same time. He says, "No, that is probably caused by stress." Knowing that David never lets anything trouble him for long, I do not think this probable at all. When we state that he is not the type to have stress. The doctor replies, "Well, migraines do not have to be caused by stress." Abandoning this circular reasoning, I ask if there is anything else that could cause these symptoms. He turns quite white and I can tell that I have made him very angry. Evidently, even if it is only a possible diagnosis, one is not allowed to question it. His answer, nothing that he knows.

By the next afternoon, one week after the trip to the hospital, David makes an amazing turnaround. We feel very relieved, certain that the very strange "virus" has passed. He begins acting almost back to normal though tired, weak, and complaining of sore legs. Again, we think that we have let him overdo. Within a couple of days, he starts vomiting and complaining of a sore throat, an earache, and a headache. This does seem like a normal virus, and we assume that his resistance has been lowered by his illness, except periodically the perplexing short chest pains occur. The pediatrician prescribes some Amoxicillin for the earache, and we wait for the customary healing.

After a few mediocre days, the illness strikes again with full force. It seems obvious that the antibiotic is not helping[1] and that this is more than an ordinary ear infection. This time, the chest pain, headache, and

---

[1] Is it really obvious that the antibiotics are not working? See Jarisch-Herxheimer reaction, footnote page 40.

dizziness cause even more concern. The doctors could not discover the cause before; it seems certain they will still have a difficult time. What can we do? Stay home and possibly watch him die? Arriving at the emergency room, the chest pain has stopped so we ask to see the renowned internist who performed the endoscopy thinking that perhaps this doctor who is so well respected by his colleagues can help us. Dr. Hardman[1] marches in and after perfunctory greetings announces that David is a major psychotic. We gasp, "No." This evokes the pronouncement, "You want your son to have a brain tumor." Shocked beyond measure, we deny this too. Smugly, he states, "Well, maybe not overtly." All this is transpiring in front of our ill, ten-year-old son. Struggling to understand what this man is saying and why, I ask, "Then you think he needs to see a psychiatrist?" Dr. Hardman blithely replies, "No, they won't do a bit of good." My own opinions of Freudian psychiatry do not reflect well, but his rejection of it puzzles me greatly. Furious at the doctor who had referred us to him, he mutters insults under his breath and demands, "Why did he send you to me?" Inexplicably, he is enraged that we have David in a wheelchair, and he caustically remarks, "I have children with meningeal tumors who aren't in wheelchairs." In further conversation, it becomes apparent that he is trying to inflict pain. After I ask several questions about different illnesses that I had read about, he sarcastically growls, "Well, you should have been a doctor." Trying to maintain some modicum of calm and lowering my pride even further than it had already been plunged, I essentially beg, "Couldn't you run some cultures or something?" His flippant reply, "Sure, which ones? "Waves of inadequacy and despair rush over me and I bleakly whisper, "I don't know." Finally I ask what is causing the 101.3 temperature. He automatically states, "He is not running a temperature." I assert positively, "Yes. He is." When he continues to deny this possibility, I realize that the man is calling me a liar. To end the argument I attest, "Look, I didn't take it. The emergency room nurse did." Angrily, he mutters, "I'll go check." Pulling out the paperwork, I point to the notation by the nurse. This produces silence for about thirty seconds. Then quickly recovering, he dismisses this as unimportant, remonstrating, "Temperature is not important. Why, several years ago we didn't even take temperatures. A kid can have a virus[2] every day of the week." Anytime

---

[1] This is a fictitious name.
[2] Definition of Virus: Latin for your guess is as good as mine.

kids start having viruses every week, you are going to have mothers camped out on the doctor's doorstep. And, furthermore, if temperatures are not important, then why do doctors and hospitals (including his office) spend so much money paying nurses to do busywork? The man is not being rational. He grabs David by the shoulders and shakes him vigorously. With all the technology available to modern medicine, this primitive test is being used to determine if my son truly has a headache. Most mothers I know could devise a better test than this. In fact, they do everyday. After this his comments vacillate between, "He looks psychotic," and "He looks sick." He definitely looks sick. How do most kids look and act with 101.3 temperature and a terrible headache? And I find myself puzzling, "What does a psychotic look like? After all, Ted Bundy <u>looked</u> pretty good to me." Questioning whether our insurance will cover it, he offers to put him in the hospital and order some physical therapy. Again, our insurance is being used as a threat. Do doctors do this all the time? Do ordinary people allow this? If our son needs medical care, insurance or no insurance, he will get it. We would gladly sell everything we own to save our son's life. Nothing of material value even begins to compare to the value of our son's life. Knowing the up and down pattern of this illness, we refuse his disinclined offer of hospitalization. Quite possibly, he could be better tomorrow, physical therapy or no physical therapy. If David experienced one of his turnarounds, the doctor would be more convinced than ever that he is right. Also, I am not a masochist. I do not wish to be in this man's presence ever again. Angrily, he remarks, "You don't like anything any of the doctors have had to say." Tears form and begin to spill over. Brokenly, I explain, "But nothing they say has made sense. I know that one needs a good relationship with a doctor--" My tears incense him even more. Disdainfully, he peers down at me from his superior intellectual position, commenting, "Look at her. She can't take care of him. We better put him in the hospital." Frank steps in at this point and defends me saying, "She has been just fine through all of this-- just fine." Hurriedly, I outwardly compose myself. Was he threatening to take my child? As a final question, I wonder quite seriously, "Are you ever wrong?" Dr. Hardman then waxes eloquent and we hear our first speech on the "art of medicine." After much reflection, I have concluded that much of the "art" involved in medicine is of the "impressionistic" variety and that, in fact, medicine is merely an **imperfect** science conducted by *imperfect* human beings who rely heavily on *imperfect* tests and ongoing research and theories.

Hurt and confused, we drag ourselves home to lick our wounds. I crawl into bed crying, image after image of David's childhood playing through my mind. The other children come and try to comfort Mom with soft, little pats and kisses. I try to explain that the doctor thought that David was faking. Jonathan immediately plants his sturdy five-year-old body on two widely-spaced feet, clenches his fists at his side, and, with blazing eyes and flushed cheeks, begins to defend his hero, his big brother. Staunchly, he proclaims, "He is not!" Somewhere deep inside myself, I smile at the picture and wonder if the doctors would believe his five-year-old innocence more than my own assertions. He and Lisa are terribly confused. Mom rarely cries and a doctor made her cry? They immediately begin thinking of this man in terms of a Hitler or Mussolini. I know that tomorrow I must explain to them that this man is very unhappy or he could not hurt other people so easily, but right now I am just too tired. How could he hurt an innocent ten-year-old child? Maybe he was angry with Frank and me for some unknown reason. But David, why hurt David? And why was he angry with us? The only explanation that seems remotely possible is that we disagreed with his diagnosis. That seems incredible. Was it because we are Christians? We find out later that he is an agnostic. This is not surprising considering his rather unorthodox and unprofessional command that we not pray. How he knew that we did is still unclear. All night long, I replay the scenes from his office trying to piece together a reasonable explanation for what happened. All night long, I recall the ten precious years of David's life. Nothing the man said about our son reconciled with my own intimate knowledge of him. And the doctor had very little knowledge at his disposal. He had run no psychological tests. All the assertions that he made were based on the fact that the blood tests and physical examination showed very little. I wish fervently that we were back in California with our pediatrician for the last six years. She is so competent and such a pleasant person to be around. Surely back at Stanford we would not be treated with such callousness. What are we going to do now? Is there a doctor in this whole city who will listen to us? Is my son going to die before someone actually believes us?

Frank is sleeping peacefully; I envy him his ability to shove things out of his mind. This has been very difficult for him as he is now in flight school upgrading to captain. Having a very sick child, listening to irate doctors, and living with an upset wife is not conducive to quiet, concentrated study. In addition to this, he has been having terrible sinus headaches requiring trips to the doctor himself for antibiotics; and every pipe in the house seems to have sprung a plumbing leak. We have always divided up the chores in a very traditional way. For the most part, Frank took care of the lawn and cars, and I took care of the house and the children. The children's medical care has always been primarily my job. I am the one who knows who is allergic to what, when they last had their inoculations, and all the other little details that mothers store in their heads. So, now I feel that it is my responsibility to find a solution to this problem without bothering him too much. He has his own responsibilities to contend with. Dear Lord, what am I to do?

Mechanically, I perform my chores the next day doing only what has to be done. All my energy and thoughts remain focused on the child suffering in the room down the hall. My neighbor sends over the article on Lyme disease again. I read it carefully still not believing that this can be related in any way. Finally, I make another doctor's appointment, this time with someone who agrees with our philosophies, beliefs, and values.

Dr. Newton[1] is very cordial and listens intently to our story. After Dr. Hardman's cutting remarks, I do not use any notes, reciting the events of the month long ordeal from memory. At the end, Dr. Newton comments, "Wow, that is some history." After carefully examining David, he feels that he has a sinus infection and attributes the chest pains to something akin to growing pains. I ask him about Lyme disease, saying, "Wouldn't the antibiotics from the appendectomy have killed it?" He answers affirmatively. Satisfied and somewhat mollified, we leave hoping against hope that this is the answer.

It is the middle of the soccer season, and David is playing his first game. He is feeling better since his doctor's visit yesterday though he still looks very pale and painfully thin. He has not gained back the ten pounds that he

---

[1] To protect identities this name also has been changed.

lost with the appendectomy, and he was wiry before it. He never was still long enough to gain any weight. With him looking better and at least out playing, the fear clutching my heart loosens its grip a tiny bit .

FOUR DAYS LATER

Despite all the ibuprofen and four days on the antibiotic, David is running an even higher temperature.[1] Lying in his bed shivering, he has stripped off his clothes trying to force his temperature to subside so that he can play in his soccer game tonight. He is begging me to let him play anyway and as much as I want him to play for he has missed so much, I have to say no. Dr. Newton seems concerned about the temperature and wants to admit David to the hospital for tests. We are terribly opposed after our abusive treatment, but we want the tests desperately. We agree.

The doubt and disbelief are evident almost as soon as the first examination begins. One doctor asks, "And just which symptom did you want us to treat, Ma'am?" Trying hard to think of an appropriate reply to such an inflammatory question, I remain silent until he rephrases the question somewhat. Then I calmly reply, "I just want my kid back."

Ostensibly, David was admitted for tests, but it soon becomes aapparentthat the blood tests and X rays could have been performed on an outpatient basis. The real reason for our admission is observation; to me, it feels like spying. When am I being a bad mother? When I am holding his hand trying to comfort him or when I am quietly joking trying to make him forget the pain? Both episodes are charted. The description of David as "reticent" is ludicrous; it is so out of character. When told of this, friends and relatives ask in amazement, "David?" Eating the food off his practically untouched tray garners me the accusation of stealing his food and not giving him the chance to eat. Struggling mightily with my escalating, boiling temper, I play the doctor game and answer their irrelevant questions. And somehow the careful answers I give are often incorrectly transcribed on the chart. While trying to dispel their doubts about his emotional wellbeing, I painstakingly explain that on the few

[1] Again, though we do not realize it, this is consistent with a Jarisch-Herxheimer reaction (see footnote page 40) and we discontinue the antibiotics.

days sprinkled here and there that he feels well, he jumps into all his activities with his normal enthusiasm and energy. This results in the notation, "Though complaining of a headache, child is going about his normal daily activities."

I begin to feel like a small insect trapped in a bottle frantically beating my wings against the glass seeking an escape. The indifferent onlookers gaze at my struggles without compassion or concern totally intent on their own probing investigation and experiments. I remember the frogs we dissected in biology class, cutting them open while still alive so that we could watch their hearts beat. With my heart exposed, I am no more important than that frog.

The doctors seem to be taking a multiple choice test in which the three obvious answers have been eliminated and the fourth, psychological, is gleefully being pounced upon as the correct answer. With the tenacity of a junk yard dog guarding a bone, they are defending their choice. The difficulty lies in that this problem is not from a medical book; it is from Life's book. And a wrong answer will not result in merely a lower grade but in possible harm to my son.

One of the hospital volunteers brings by a watercolor set and I watch as my normally animated son finally finds something creative to occupy his time that he can still physically accomplish. Splashing colors on the cardboard, he remarks with surprise, "I never knew painting could be so much fun." What he means is that he has never been bored enough or still long enough to try it. Coloring papers were always done at the speed of lightning so as to move on to more exciting, important activities. This hustle and bustle of activity has not gone unnoticed by others. In kindergarten, he was given a certificate for "Most Creative." This was mainly due to his rather unusual "Show and Tell" antics. Thankfully, the pictures are of birds, butterflies, flowers, and trees and done in bright blues, reds, yellows, and greens. If the subjects had been snakes, spiders, and bats done in black (which, with David, could quite easily have happened), I am certain that it could have been entered into the chart with dire observations. As it is, one doctor seems quite taken with the sheet he used to clean his brush. She questions him carefully trying to find a hidden meaning and tells him to his amazement that this is her favorite.

While I am grateful that David has something to do, it only seems to highlight the strange and complete transformation that has overtaken my son. For almost ten years now on a daily basis, I have made comments like, "David, be still!", "David, don't jump (run, climb, sling, throw, etc.) in the house," and "David, it is someone else's turn to talk." Now that he is so very still and quiet, I wish for the irritation. I want my active, healthy son back! I want my kid who cannot walk through the house without jumping to hit the door frames and who tells childish jokes and riddles continually. How can I fight the strange prejudices that surround us?

After explaining to Dr. Newton's associate that Dr. Newton had promised to run a Lyme test, the doctor asks if David was bitten by a tick. When I reply in the affirmative, he raises his eyebrows and skeptically queries, "Really, when?" I gaze at him steadily and succinctly state, "In August." (Actually, where we live if one spends any time at all outdoors in July and August, the challenge is to **not** be bitten.) He says, "Well, we need to know because we run a different test depending on the length of time since the tick bite." At the time, I accept this explanation. With more education, I will realize that there is no truth to this statement. There are no tests divided in such a way. Another doctor with whom I had spoken on the phone had suggested that perhaps a spinal tap might give us some more information. So, rather hesitantly, I ask, "Do you think that perhaps he might need a spinal tap?" The doctor explodes, "Good g--, no! His neck is as supple as yours and mine." On his way out, I watch in amazement as he stops to administer a variation of the shaking test; bouncing David hard on the bed, he watches his reaction to check the veracity of his headache. Is this what doctors are learning in med school? Have I fallen down the rabbit hole? It would not surprise me at any moment to see a large, white rabbit hopping into the room, shouting, "I'm late. I'm late--for a very important date."

On a niceness scale, I would rate our family way above average. As far as I know, we do not have one enemy in this entire world. Frank is especially very slow to take offense and refuses for the most part to argue with anyone. Once when a fellow co-pilot was complaining about a particularly obnoxious captain, Frank shrugged his shoulders and said, "Oh, I got along with him just fine." To which the other pilot smiled and laughingly stated, "Frank, you could get along with Attila the Hun."

THE MYSTERIOUS ILLNESS

Normally, our policy when disagreeing with someone is to drop the subject. We refuse to argue about unimportant or irresolvable matters. When a doctor told me to open my windows in January because my house was probably too hot, I did not argue with him, but neither did I heed his advice. (We later found that Jonathan had asthma and opening the windows would probably have only increased his problems.) However, when our child's life hangs in the balance, we cannot just go home and pretend that these people do not exist. How have we managed to entangle ourselves in such an impossible situation?

David's temperature is receding, and with it and the mostly normal test results go any doubts that the doctors may have had about their diagnosis. The "nonspecific" sedimentation rate is still elevated and one doctor inanely asks, "Does he always have an elevated sedimentation rate?" How many mothers do you know who take their well children in for regular sedimentation rate checks? Well aware of their erroneous conclusions, I plead for answers trying to appeal to their logic, saying, "Let's assume that he is telling the truth. What **could** cause these symptoms?" Their answer, "Nothing that we are familiar with." Rather arrogantly the doctor tells us, "We thought of calling in some more specialists, but since we could not find anything we do not figure they could either." Pragmatically she adds, "He will either get better, worse, or remain the same. " Astounded, we leave the hospital for the third time.

When the children were younger, I used to astonish Frank with my ability to deduce that the children were running a temperature. Out of the clear blue, I would tell him that one was sick; and when the temperature was read, he would look at me genuinely puzzled and say, "How did you know?" Now though I enjoyed this immensely, I truly did not think that I had any magical powers. It was simply that I spent so much time observing them, that when something was not quite right, I noticed it. Mothers become quite adept at noticing long silences, soft janglings that indicate a forbidden object is being touched or, most especially, ominous splashing sounds coming from the bathroom. We also spend a considerable amount of time examining small faces for telltale evidence of minor crimes. Endlessly we ask the question, "What do you have in your mouth?" We breathe a sigh of relief when they answer, "Did you know that blue crayon tastes good, Mommy?" and gasp when they answer, "I found three mushrooms in the backyard." (This particular revelation necessitated a fast trip to the emergency room, and David vowed never to eat mushrooms again.) Who but a mother would have known when nine month old David began frantically screaming "fire" at bedtime that it was not fire, but 'fier, pacifier. Who else could have known that "deeka" meant blanket? Who else knows my children as well as I do? When children exhibit what to others would be insignificant behavior, a mother notices. For centuries when a child's eyes appear slightly sunken and their face a little pale or flushed, mothers have instinctively known that something was wrong. Experiments have even shown that a mother is able to distinguish her baby's cries from others, and babies are able to recognize their mother's voice and smell. Perhaps God has heightened our senses in a special way to enable us to protect these small creatures placed in our care. My child is sick. How do I convince the doctors of something that I innately just know?

Coming home from yet another doctor visit (I estimate that we have seen twenty-five or so), David appears to be deep in thought. Puzzled he asks, "Mom, can a person really make himself sick without knowing it?" All the accusations by the doctors are beginning to make him wonder. Sighing, not sure if I even believe the answer I am giving, I reply, "Yes, if he is very worried or upset about something." Satisfied, he matter-of-factly pronounces, "Well, that's out then."

Each doctor visit is a torturous experience for me. I now expect doctors to have a Dr. Jekyll and Mr. Hyde personality, and, even if one is nice to us extrinsically, I am still petrified of Dr. Jekyll's transformation to Mr. Hyde. I am suspicious of the notes that they surreptitiously copy into their charts and am much too intimidated to return to one, if on the first visit they do not indicate that they have some idea what is wrong. Because we have an HMO for the moment and a primary care physician who has grown very weary of us, all of these extra visits are being paid for out of our own pockets. But the money is very minor compared to the emotional upheaval that is produced with each visit as I armor myself to ward off the expected insults and tirades.

Back at home, I have the gas company test our house for carbon monoxide leaks and buy a radon tester. I call our pediatrician in California, hoping that she will have some idea of how to proceed. When I tell her that his back and thigh have started going numb, she insists that he needs to see the neurologist again. When I call the neurologist, he refuses to see us. The hospital grapevine is working well. I say, "Then you are not concerned about the numbness?" He replies, "I did not say that." No, he did not precisely say it, but that is exactly what he meant. Though we have not lost our temper with anyone even with the extreme provocation of Dr. Hardman, we have been labeled as trouble.

Dr. Hardman seems to have built a reputation for being "outspoken" and "blunt." The other doctors are well aware of it but dismiss his "bedside manner" as unimportant in comparison to his great diagnostic ability. If a doctor is told of our treatment before his name is mentioned, they are horrified. When his name is mentioned, they become very quiet. He must have a tremendous amount of power in the medical community. It seems to be an example of, "Absolute power corrupts absolutely." How sad that a man can behave in such a reprehensible manner and receive no censure at all from his colleagues. I do not blame the doctors for not being able to discover the cause of the illness, but I do not understand how they can be so callous to people who are already hurting tremendously. We have no one to help us; no one who will even look for a cause. We are **alone** in this terrifying battle.

When we tell our friends and relatives, their reactions are much the same. The women say emphatically, "I would sue." and the men say wonderingly, "I would have hit him. How <u>did</u> you keep from it?" Actually, looking back on it, we feel it was God's restraint and nothing of ourselves. If Frank had hauled back and hit him, he would probably be in jail. And to sue would hurt us much more than him. Obviously, he is very hardened, but we are not. The things that he could say and do in a court case could continue to hurt us especially the children if they were required to testify. In any case, we have decided upon a much more effective way of dealing with Dr. Hardman--prayer. God has ways and means of touching people that we know not. Together, the children and we, have been praying for his salvation. This has helped us to let go of the problem and turn it over to One who can do all things.

The symptoms come and go with the ease of a zephyr wreaking havoc in our lives and leaving little telltale evidence. Most of the time now David refuses to leave his bed. Even enticements such as watching his favorite team, the Oakland A's, play in the World Series cannot budge him. He now remains in a darkened room lying flat on his back unable to bear any loud noises. The headache is so severe that he cannot read or watch television. Pathetically, he implores me to think of something he can do. Afraid of masking an important symptom, we are giving him no pain relievers of any kind. When the hour long chest pains occur, he pleads with us to take him to the doctor saying that it feels like an elephant is sitting on his chest. Grimly, our hearts breaking, we refuse knowing it will accomplish nothing. The pain is so bad that I cannot imagine it not being an emergency situation, but, to the doctors, it is not. How will I, with my complete lack of medical expertise, know when the situation crosses the line and becomes a medical emergency that the doctors can recognize?

At night, sleep haplessly eludes me; I pad softly down the hall time and time again to ensure that he is still breathing. When I do sleep, nightmares pervade. Over and over, I see myself carrying his limp, lifeless body back to the disbelieving, indifferent doctors.

Lord Jesus, you can hear my groanings that cannot be uttered. I do not know where to go or who to turn to. I am so tired. Please, I beg you, please, help our family.

At every cross-way on the road
that leads to the future,
Tradition
has placed against each of us,
ten-thousand men to guard the
Past.

      Maurice Masterlinck
      1907

OCCAM'S RAZOR

A guiding principle of science stating that the simplest
hypothesis accounting for the most facts is the most
likely to be correct.

      William of Occam
       14th century English scholastic philosopher

CHAPTER FOUR

Could It Really Be Lyme?

Carefully, I read and reread the Lyme disease article underlining and practically memorizing portions of it. Certain phrases begin to jump out, "only sixty percent have rashes," "symptoms and onset of symptoms vary widely," and, importantly, "doctors have a difficult time diagnosing it." At my insistence, a Lyme titer was run before we left the hospital; but I am reluctant to hope after reading about the inaccuracies and inconsistencies of the test. "A negative Lyme titer does not mean that you do not have Lyme disease. Lyme disease is a clinical diagnosis." Listing David's symptoms, (severe headache, stiff neck, ear pain, throat pain, dizziness, difficulty walking, elevated liver enzymes, elevated sedimentation rate, gastritis, fever, photosensitivity, noise sensitivity, nausea, chest pains, numbness) I note that all of them are encompassed by the amazing number of Lyme symptoms. It is the first and only illness I have found that could account for these symptoms comprehensively. I have tried going to the library and searching through medical books. Though I can basically understand them with the aid of a medical dictionary, the process is time consuming and awkward. I need someone who already has the knowledge to help me now. Tomorrow may be too late.

When the doctor calls with the negative Lyme titer, I am prepared. Mentioning the test's problems, I ask about the possibility of David having Lyme. He states that he does not have the symptoms. When I ask, "Which symptoms?" He replies, "He did not have a rash." I present my statistic of only sixty per cent developing the rash. He answers with an old medical maxim, "When you hear hoof beats, you don't look for zebras." (Now, that might apply to some situations, but ticks are not confined to zoos. And if you see stripes, you better start looking for zebras.) He begins telling me what a fine doctor the neurologist we saw is. I agree. He then goes on to tell me that, despite his problems, Dr. Hardman is also a fine doctor. The words slam into the pit of my stomach and knock the air from my lungs. They ping-pong inside my head as trembling I fight for control. A fine doctor? To me, this is tantamount to telling a rape victim that her rapist is a fine, upstanding citizen. Without compassion, a doctor is something less than a doctor. A bedside manner is part and parcel of the same package. At my continued insistence that perhaps Lyme could be the problem, Dr. Newton seems genuinely puzzled, remarking, "You sound desperate." Helplessly, I admit, "That's right. I am desperate." Then replacing the phone in its cradle, I cry.

This doctor wants nothing more to do with us. He feels that we should see a psychiatrist. We are at an impasse. Finally, believing that it is the only way to silence their fears about his mental health, I have agreed but only with the stipulation that the psychiatrist be a Christian. After several college classes in the subject, I have no confidence in many of the theories and preposterous notions that Freud and Jung seem to have foisted on the whole human race as fact. The thought of someone whose beliefs are in total antithesis to ours manipulating our son's mind and emotions while he is so vulnerably incapacitated is frightening. One who is a Christian will at least have some common ground with us, but, even so, we have no reason to believe that this doctor will be any more discerning than the others.

After days of searching, they have been unable to find a Christian psychiatrist who sees children. The pediatrician is adamant that only a psychiatrist will do, not a psychologist. Frank and I are secretly relieved. We had not wanted to pursue this course anyway; and watching David deteriorate in the meantime, we do not feel that we have the time to waste.

Though I may not be able to discuss many subjects on the same level as a doctor, I am convinced that on the subject of my children's mental heath I can speak with a greater authority than anyone on the planet. None of these doctors would attempt to guess my son's hematocrit or white blood cell count without a test. Why do they attempt to guess at his mental condition based on nothing more than a lack of physical test confirmation? Do they honestly believe a child would go completely crazy just because he move across the country? And if they do really believe this, then why are they not at least somewhat sympathetic? A child in enough mental anguish to fabricate such bizarre symptoms and to punish himself by staying in bed and missing activities must be truly in great pain. I begin to wonder if there are any real psychological illnesses that exhibit physical symptoms; perhaps there are just physical illnesses that doctors cannot recognize. I think of people with Alzheimer's disease and parents of children with autism. These too were told that it was a mental illness until medical science could *prove* differently.

Searching for answers, I begin making numerous phone calls. The Centers for Disease Control have thirty cases of Lyme on record for the state of Tennessee last year. Interestingly, this is up from thirteen cases the previous year and only one was reported the year before that. The county health department has two cases reported for last year, but it is possible that they were contracted out of state. Also, in trying to determine what qualifies as a reportable case of Lyme disease, I realize that the CDC definition varies quite widely from the actual disease process as described in the medical journals. The person that I talk to says that they are aware of the problems with the test and the absence of the rash in many cases, but that they must have irrefutable evidence to count a case. They are aware that this results in numerous unreported cases of Lyme perhaps as many as nine or ten unreported cases for every one that is.

When I discover that the disease is spread by migratory birds and that the ticks will feed on thirty mammals and fifty species of birds, I am more puzzled than ever by the doctor's insistence that there is no Lyme Disease here. Does Tennessee have some sort of magic shield protecting it from infiltration by the infected ticks? Logically, it seems to me that even one person moving in from out of state with an infected pet could spread the disease. Why are they so insistent in their assertions that the disease is not here? And, furthermore, unbeknownst to me, California, the state we had just left, has a very high rate of this disease.

Calling the Lyme Borreliosis Foundation in Tolland, Connecticut, I am referred to a Dr. Ed Masters, in Cape Girardeau, Missouri. They indicate that he is much respected in this field and an excellent physician. Feeling slightly strange to be calling a doctor hours away when there are hundreds in this city, I place the call.

Dr. Masters' waiting room is filled with pictures of his children and newspaper articles. The smiling faces of his four lovely children reassure me. How could anyone have four kids, not the prescribed 1.8, and not genuinely like children? We peruse the articles on the wall thoughtfully. He is a walnut tree farmer, and, in fact, researching a speech for the Walnut Growers Association is how he became aware of the Lyme disease problem in Missouri in the first place. Raised on a farm myself, my experience has led me to think of farmers, for the most part, as honest, hard working, and God-fearing people. So, though not precisely the same kind of farmer as those with whom I was acquainted, this also is a plus in his favor. A magazine article written by him describes the suffering of a patient with Alzheimer's, and you can sense his pain as toward the end of the article he unveils the identity of the patient, his mother. He must have loved his mother deeply, a definite plus. One plaque reveals that he possesses a patent on a needle which he and another fellow developed indicating a certain amount of ingenuity. We also read a poem he has authored analogizing drugs to a female black widow spider who in the end consumes her mate. Does this doctor have the compassion and resourcefulness, so woefully lacking in the other doctors, to help our son?

After reviewing the facts of our case, Dr. Masters informs us that David has classic[1] Lyme symptoms and that he is putting him on antibiotics, hefty doses of Amoxicillin, probably for a period of six months. His nurse, Pam, spends a great deal of time explaining the disease and the problems with the test results. A victim of Lyme herself, she is dedicated to increasing awareness of the illness. We are cautiously optimistic and leave clutching the precious prescription of high dosage antibiotics.

---

[1] Emphasis mine. Since that time other doctors have also called these classic Lyme symptoms.

CHAPTER FIVE

A Reprieve

The world is sunny, warm, bright, and beautiful again. David is doing well, and we feel confident that the diagnosis and treatment are correct. After five days on the antibiotic, David improved dramatically and most importantly the improvement has continued. He is gradually regaining his strength and beginning to eat like a horse again. The trees are arrayed in their glorious fall colors: magenta, orange, and gold; and with hearts relieved of a great burden, we delight in the renewed pleasure of their beauty. The children pile huge stacks of leaves and laughingly jump in. Tentatively, we flex our wings and resume our normally busy lifestyle.

When we return to Dr. Masters after a month, we find that David's Lyme test surprisingly enough has come back positive. Actually, it is a very high equivocal, a borderline. But the Western Blot is read individually, and there is a margin for error in the interpretation so that Dr. Masters feels it easily could have been read positive, especially with David's symptoms. The diagnosis is confirmed by the archaic and unreliable test. Though a negative test means nothing in Lyme disease with such a high percentage of false negatives, a positive Western Blot is an entirely different matter. There is only a one percent false positive rate.

Our gratitude toward Dr. Masters is overwhelming and inexpressible. After experiencing the scorn of other doctors, one who could and would help is a striking contrast. Every day I find myself thanking God for leading us to him and for the miracle of antibiotics. Only having used antibiotics for minor illnesses such as sore throats and ear infections, we had not observed the dramatic improvement of someone who is seriously ill and had taken their lifesaving abilities so much for granted. I promise myself that never again will I take life's small daily pleasures frivolously. Watching David's young, strong limbs pump vigorously around the gymnasium playing basketball brings immense satisfaction. My eyes fill with tears when I remember the sick, pitiful waif of a few weeks ago. His coordination has improved over last year, and the wild energy that he displayed then is now more controlled and graceful. He is so full of life.

The children's confidence in doctors (not to mention my own) has been badly shaken. When I tell Jonathan that I think that he may have a cavity and that he is going to have to go the dentist, his first question is not, "Will it hurt?" but, "Will the doctor yell at me?" I know that I must do something to remove at least some of the tarnish from the doctors' reputations. I have always at opportune times suggested various careers to my children. So, while studying math one day, I casually mention that if they should decide to become a doctor, they will need to know a lot of math. Looking at me as if I had just for all the world suggested that one day they might want to be bank robbers, they emphatically chorus, "No way, Jose." Carefully, I point out, "Well, where do you think we would be without Dr. Masters? We do need some good doctors, you know." Mulling this over a bit, they reluctantly concede that the world does need some more good doctors and that they might consider being one just like Dr. Masters.

Though still somewhat battered and scarred, the struggle with David's illness has left us feeling stronger and more confident of our ability to handle difficult situations. The intense emotions have somehow bonded us together even more tightly as a family. Jonathan with the naivety of childhood asks a question one day that highlights just how onerous the past two months have been on the whole family. He wonders, "Mom, which one of us, Lisa or me, would you rather have cancer next since David has already had his cancer?" We reassure him that we love all of them and do not want any of them to have cancer or anything else that could hurt. We do not realize that his question will have a prophetic element.

CHAPTER SIX

The Enemy Strikes Again

A niggling fear is buzzing around inside my head, but, resolutely, I brush it aside, determined that nothing mar this first Christmas in Tennessee. Finally, our tree is up and decorated. The kids had almost given up hope. Things are moving a little slow this year. We are still playing catch up on all the things that were shoved aside to deal with the illness. The shopping is basically completed, a minor miracle of itself. We are going to my Mom's for an early Christmas celebration. We have not been to Oklahoma for Christmas in over ten years because Frank's job usually does not permit traveling at that time, so this is a highly anticipated trip.

Lisa has been complaining of a headache and her knees hurting for a couple of weeks now. As it has not slowed her down much I basically have been ignoring it thinking it just a holdover from the bad virus she had. Hopefully, Christmas break will allow her enough rest to be back in full swing by the first of the year.

By the end of the visit with my Mom, there is no longer any way to ignore Lisa's symptoms. She is feeling much worse and noticeably limping. Going up and down stairs has become almost impossible. My suspicion's are heightened, and we decide to all submit to Lyme testing after the Christmas holidays. The rest of us have also been experiencing some strange sensations. I do not want to over-react though we all were bitten by ticks back in August when we first arrived. Lyme disease is supposed to be fairly rare as only three to five percent of the ticks in this area have been found to carry the disease spirochete. Still I have no explanation for the strange headaches, nausea, joint pain, and stabbing, shooting pains that have begun plaguing our family.

Christmas Day is always a happy celebration of Jesus' birth in our family. Oftentimes, we do not celebrate on the actual day because Frank's job forces him to be out of town. One year he missed every holiday in the entire year. This is a very special Christmas because he is actually home, but even so the day seems sadly lacking in luster and excitement. The boys do not seem to notice anything amiss. They are delighted with their gifts and especially excited by the white stuff on the ground outside. It is our first white Christmas; in San Jose it never snowed. Though much too icy to be called proper snow, it is very satisfactory to two little boys who had never before played in anything like it. Wistfully, Lisa gazes out the window watching the wild romping boys throwing snowballs and making angel wings. We remind her that David missed a lot of activities just a month or so ago and that she will probably be well real soon. Though she realizes this, it is still a big disappointment and so is missing the junior high church activities scheduled over the holidays.

I am feeling perfectly rotten myself and this does not make life any easier. With both the girls in the family feeling under the weather, cooking and cleaning slow down quite a bit. I manage to cook Christmas dinner without my usual cheerful helper and open gifts, but then I go to bed. We seem to be consuming ibuprofen and Drixoral at an astonishing rate. Frank says that if we keep having sinus this bad in Tennessee, we will have to move. I had promised Frank that I would make pecan pies. After all, Christmas is not Christmas without pecan pies. But no matter how I try to force myself to make those pies, I cannot seem to work up the energy to do so. The very thought of pecan pie makes me ill. Nothing has been tasting right lately. This dreadful nausea will not go away and I am so tired. Actually, I feel just like I did when I was pregnant, but I know I am not. Maybe I will buy a pregnancy test just to be sure. Every evening my temperature seems to rise and then I feel worse than ever. Did I have a temperature during my other pregnancies? I cannot remember.

We have an appointment for January 4 with Dr. Masters, but we decide that maybe we should not wait that long for a doctor's opinion. We are still very leery of doctors especially in this city, but we nonetheless take Lisa in. The only way to completely avoid doctors is to stay healthy. This does not seem to be an option in our case. I have been wondering if the mild case of scoliosis that she has could be causing any of her problems. The doctor examines her knees and finds nothing visibly wrong with them. Since I have concerns about the scoliosis, he recommends that I see an orthopedist. The fact that David has Lyme disease evokes no response.

We only have an appointment for David on the fourth, and I know of no other way to see the doctor when he is so far away. So, reluctantly, regretting the inconvenience, I ask for the blood testing for the rest of the family. I do not realize what a time consuming prospect this will be thinking the doctor need only order them. Dr. Masters is very thorough though and examines each of us making him and his staff very late leaving his office. He does not feel our symptoms are severe enough to warrant treating at this time. I do ask for antibiotics for Lisa but not very forcefully. The other doctors have left an indelible impression on my mind.

The orthopedist back at home can find nothing in his field that would explain her symptoms. He refers us to a rheumatologist. This doctor seems quite interested in the fact that her brother has Lyme disease and is more knowledgeable on the subject than most I have met here. I am impressed that he at least seems to realize that there is a problem with the testing. By the time we see this doctor, the joint pain has spread to her ankles, wrists, elbows, and fingers. Now, in addition, to giving up all her athletic endeavors, she must also relinquish one of her most enjoyable activities, the piano. Even carrying a heavy glass has become an impossibility. She is becoming more and more incapacitated.

We go out to eat after this appointment. I had not envisioned how hard it would be. I cringe as people stare pityingly wondering what is wrong as we support her limping painfully to the table. Always before, people had watched her lithe, graceful body with admiration, and when the children were smaller it was more common than not to receive compliments on our beautiful children. I think of all the handicapped children that I have seen in my lifetime. My heart always went out to them, but no matter how much you pity someone, you cannot imagine the pain of living with something like this and suddenly being the recipient of the pity.

It has been two weeks since our Lyme tests so I call for the results. Unhappily, all of our tests are negative. However, after hearing how much worse Lisa has become, Dr. Masters puts her on a trial course of antibiotics. So, very relieved, I expect to see improvement in five or six days as we did with David.

By midmorning of the next day, Lisa goes to bed and only rises to go to the bathroom. She is feeling much worse. Dr. Masters had warned us of what they called a Herxheimer[1] reaction in which there is a worsening of symptoms. She is definitely much worse. Her headache and joint pain are worse, and she is having sharp, stabbing pains that shift from joint to joint. Alternately, she will feel burning hot and then cold. She will say she is having "hot chills." This is tough to watch, but we expect the worst to be over in a few days.

Lisa has made quite a few friends considering the short while that we have lived here. Her basketball team is especially concerned as she has missed all but the first two games. The entire team makes plans for a visit. Although the prospect of their visit buoys her spirits all day, the actual visit is short when they glimpse the expressions on her face as she struggles to suppress and conceal the small whimpers that escape as the pain suddenly stabs another joint with ferocity. They stare at the trophy collection on her bureau and then at the girl in the bed. The strong, active girl they knew is in total contradiction with this invalid.

Finally, with much reluctance, we take another step down the spiral staircase. We rent a wheelchair. Though believing this to be a temporary inconvenience, it is still heartrending. Somehow there is an ominous sense of foreboding associated with this ugly, metal, mechanical contraption. It is an unwelcome necessity just to transport her back and forth to doctor visits.

Pushing that wheelchair produces a horrible tension within me. As the heads swivel toward us, I steel myself and pushing even faster refuse to even glance into any of the curious faces. I wish we were invisible and unreasonably want to scream, "Quit looking at us. Leave us alone." Is this

---

[1] Jarisch-Herxheimer reactions occur soon after starting antibiotics and are immunologic reactions to the sudden release of large amounts of bacterial antigen as the spirochetes are destroyed. This causes chills, fever, increased joint pain, rashes, rapid heart rate, and rapid respirations.

really my child in this unnatural position? Am I really pushing this thing? This happens to other people, not us.

After ten days, she is still no better. We are worried and concerned. Dr. Masters thinks that it is just a particularly bad Herxheimer reaction, but even if it is juvenile rheumatoid arthritis, there is some literature to support antibiotic therapy. The theories in medicine come and go. Years ago arthritis was thought to have an infectious agent as its root cause. The last decade or so it has been considered an auto-immune illness caused by the body attacking itself for some unknown reason. Recently, there has been some shift back to the supposition that perhaps it is in some cases after all an infectious illness.

We return to the rheumatologist for our test results. Every test is normal. This is confusing to say the least. How can a child be so very ill and absolutely nothing show up on her test results? The rheumatologist seems very upset that we now have her on antibiotics. Our feeling is no matter what is wrong, the antibiotics will not hurt. Also, there is a very, very good chance that this is Lyme and then the antibiotics could make a big difference. We had already seen just how big a difference it could make with David.

By nature, I am such a cautious person that I have never had a speeding ticket or traffic violation of any kind. Anything that even remotely resembles gambling, including the stock market, makes me uneasy. This caution extends into the area of dispensing medication especially to my children. I have never handed out even aspirin capriciously. When one of my children would say they had a headache, my stock answer was, "Well, go take a nap. You are probably tired." They rarely complained. I know that antibiotics can cause a serious allergic reaction. I lived through one with this same child. And when a doctor wanted to put her on antibiotics for six months to stop the ear infections as a five-year-old, we declined. I know, that though the list of side effects is small especially in comparison to drugs such as steroids and anti-depressants, they do exist. I love this child. I want what is best for her. And after seeing several doctors and amassing as much knowledge as I know how to acquire, every motherly instinct that I possess tells me that taking the antibiotics is the best and safest course to pursue.

This rheumatologist wants us to see a pediatric rheumatologist at the hospital where David was admitted. The very idea of returning to that place is distasteful, but we agree.

Though we have not seen this doctor or any in the rheumatology department before, the very halls seem tainted by the maltreatment we had experienced here. I determine that they will not call me an over-anxious mother and decide to do my best to appear bored and unconcerned. Though I answer their questions to the best of my ability, I do not volunteer any information, express any concern, or ask any questions. As the examination progresses, we find that every single joint in Lisa's body is causing her pain. She had not been moving around and did not realize until they moved her shoulders and hips through range of motion that these also were painful. In addition to the joint pain, the headache and flu-like malaise makes it difficult for her to sit up for any length of time. Just sitting in the wheelchair is exhausting, and she is in a great deal of pain at all times. As I somehow expected, they do not have any idea what is wrong with Lisa, but they do want to see David's Lyme test to verify that he actually has Lyme. They review the tests from the other rheumatologist and run some of their own. I am grateful that at least no psychological nonsense is brought into the picture.

CHAPTER SEVEN

The Hospital Again

In a strange dichotomy, we are relieved and yet dismayed to be in the hospital again. After three weeks on the oral antibiotics, Lisa is in such pain that she cannot sleep. The pain during the day is bad enough; pain at night is unbearable. So, thankfully, Dr. Masters is placing her in the hospital to insert a PIC[1] line and start her on IV penicillin. Our one big regret is that she cannot take the drug of choice, the cephalosporins. She had a severe allergic reactions to Ceclor as a four year old and we were told that if she ever had any of the drugs in this family it could kill her. So, the best drugs, Rocephin and Claforan, are prohibited, but we hear from several sources of individuals who responded better to the penicillin than to the cephalosporins. So, we are very optimistic. After all, she has not had this disease for years like the hard to cure cases that we hear about.

This is a different hospital, and I am hopeful that with a doctor backing us the nurses will accept this disease at face value. A couple of nurses in the hospital are being treated for Lyme, and there has been quite a bit of publicity regarding Lyme disease in this area as opposed to where we are from. In fact, the CDC has declared the southeastern corner of Missouri an endemic area for Lyme disease.

Lisa has stopped eating and drinking almost entirely. She says it hurts too much to eat. At home, we had been tempting her with her favorite ice cream, mashed potatoes (secretly mixed with eggs), homemade popsicles

---

[1] PIC--Percutaneously Inserted Catheter. This is a silastic catheter that is inserted into a deep vein. Lisa's is placed in the bend of her elbow. This type can remain in place for months as opposed to a peripheral IV which must be changed every three days. It is covered with an occlusive dressing which must be changed at least once a week. The line must be flushed with syringes daily.

made with yogurt, and creamed soups. In the hospital, it is much harder to concoct something she will eat, but we try. Though we are throwing away entire trays of untouched food, we do not so much as nibble on it until a nurse invites us to eat them. We are being very careful in this hospital trying to say and do exactly the right thing.

Our Sunday School class has been so kind and good to us. Though we barely knew these people at the onset of all this illness, it has served as an impetus to forge friendships even more quickly than normal. They have felt so badly for Lisa and us and have offered time and time again to help us. With my stubborn pride, I constantly turn down their offers, but they contrive a unique plan to cheer us up. One lady makes a huge decorative basket and then each class member contributes a gift to the basket. Lisa is to open one gift a day until they are gone. This is such a wonderful idea. That someone could have cared enough to devise and implement this idea is wonderfully comforting. One of Lisa's first requests every morning, no matter how bad the pain, is to open her present. It gives her something to look forward to each day and, for a moment, takes her mind off the pain. We feel a tremendous gratitude to these loving people and feel as though God himself has wrapped his arms around us in love.

Hurray, Lisa's Lyme test, a Western Blot, has come back positive. Eight specific IgG and IgM bands, 100, 83, 41, 39, 34, 31, 25, and 20, translate into a solid, unequivocal positive result. Smiles wreathe our faces, and mentally we are turning cartwheels. A great sense of euphoria washes over us. With this test, any doubts about the diagnosis are removed; and we feel a certainty that it is just a matter of time before she is her normal self again.

At first, we do not worry about her not eating assuming that just as with a virus or flu when she feels a little better she will eat. She has lost five or six pounds, but this does not seem like an inordinate amount. And the medicine should begin to take effect soon. After three or four days though, the nurses are becoming concerned. We begin the terrible ordeal of forcing her to eat. Every bite is painful and requires much coercion on our part. We bargain, "Three bites of mashed potatoes and two of the ice cream. That's all you have to eat." Upon being told that she would have to have a tube inserted into her stomach if she does not eat, she resignedly

THE HOSPITAL AGAIN 45

says, "Go ahead, it couldn't hurt any worse than eating." Finally after a week of this, she swallows a bite of food and a look of great surprise crosses her face. She exclaims, "That didn't hurt to swallow." We rejoice in this small yet strategic victory .

In the midst of our celebration, something extremely odd and upsetting occurs. Lisa's jaw slides uncontrollably out of position, the lower jaw jutting sideways. My first reaction is to laugh. It looks so strange. Then I realize that I cannot do that. Lisa is terribly upset and begins asking for a mirror. I refuse to give her one. The strain on her jaw is very painful, and the loss of control is inexplicably frightening. Also, as is normal for an almost teenager, she becomes very concerned about her appearance. After knocking three teeth loose with the force of the shift, she puts her retainers in and does not remove them. This happens off and on for two days and then stops. She becomes terrified of this happening again. If her jaw feels the slightest bit strange, she immediately asks for her retainers. If being afraid and stress could have caused this to happen, it should have gone on and on because her fear of this event is extreme. But, strangely enough, it leaves never to return.

The night of the jaw incident I am so emotionally upset, I cry and cry after Lisa is asleep. Each thing that happens seems like it should be the last straw, but somehow we go on. There is no other choice. The next morning my eyes feel like they have ground glass in them. I rinse them with cool water and lie down with a cold rag blocking out the light. Feeling stupid for crying and getting make-up in my eyes, I decide not to use any more make-up until they quit looking so red. I cannot afford to be incapacitated in any way. Frank is at the motel running 102 to 103 degree temperatures and experiencing horrible chills. He had continued to have joint pain, headaches, and other symptoms. One of the other symptoms caused him much concern. While flying his last trip, he could not remember the call number for the particular flight he was on. Each time he used the radio to identify his aircraft, he had to look up the number on his paperwork. This had never happened before. True, he was tired and under a lot of stress with Lisa being so ill, but he has been tired for almost every trip he has flown and has also been under a lot of stress before. Viet Nam could hardly be called a picnic. As a captain on a 727, his health is vital to him for his safety and others depends on it. So, after further evaluation, Dr. Masters put him on antibiotics two days ago. We think that now he is having a Herxheimer reaction especially as he has rashes covering his thighs. The boys are going stir crazy in a small, confined space, and Frank is having a miserable time trying to keep them quiet while he tries to rest.

It is our ninth day in the hospital. Lisa is feeling some better; she actually is smiling for the first time in weeks. Our relief is palpable, and we ready ourselves to go that most wonderful of places, HOME. Option Care comes to show us how to operate the cassette pump we will be using at home to administer Lisa's medicine. Frank and I are both still feeling like zombies. I ask him if he is understanding all this and he wants to know if I am. We both feel incredibly stupid, but the truth is we just do not physically feel well. I ask if some of this is written down because I do not think that either one of us is retaining the information.

Undoubtedly, even though Frank is feeling weak and sick, he will have to drive home. My eyes are hurting so badly I cannot bear to open them in the sunlight even with sunglasses, and, furthermore, my eyesight has weakened a great deal. Somehow I am beginning to suspect that this has something to do with Lyme disease, but I do not even want to think about seeing a doctor. Anything to do with Lyme disease seems impossible to discover with their testing, and, frankly, I just cannot bear having a doctor tell me that my eyes are fine. It is just stress. The very word stress makes me want to scream, rail, kick, bite, gnash my teeth, and vomit.

While Frank is driving, I close my eyes and ponder. Stress--what a vague, "nonspecific," all-encompassing diagnosis. One that is arrived at not on the basis of much indisputable evidence, but rather on the lack thereof. And who among us is exempt from this most prevalent, currently fashionable malady? Everything from the most serious illnesses like heart attacks and cancer to milder problems like ulcers and migraines to the totally benign "psychological" diagnosis is supposed to have stress ramifications. Now separating actual physical stresses like dietary and sleep deficiencies which in the United States are for the majority of people personal choices not necessities, we are supposed to be the most stressed out generation to have ever existed. I suppose that this means that we would all prefer to live in another time and place. But, I wonder. Would we really rather have been a pregnant, pioneer wife trudging across the plains losing a husband to the hardships of the trail? Would we rather have been a slave in the Old South groveling to the master and inwardly seething? Would we rather have been an orphan child in Charles Dickens' England suffering in the workhouses of the era? How about the soldiers and their families that fought in the multitude of wars that have continually plagued our planet? Just which time and place did you choose over where you are right now? Which point and time in history is free from this unsavory villain? It seems to me to be a very arrogant assumption that we in our comparative peace, safety, and luxury have more stress and, therefore, more stress related illnesses than any other time. Nonetheless, I have no concrete facts, only swirling opinions that crowd my brain until our mini-van finally rolls to a stop in our driveway.

Amid the frenzied cries of joy from our cocker spaniel, we stiffly disembark. The boys are delighted to be home and act like wild young animals suddenly freed from a cage. Once inside, Lisa, too, is glad to be home where it is much quieter than the hospital. We both grew to despise the shrill, infernal beeping of the IV machines. The nurses were nice, but we often speculated that they must be accustomed to speaking to deaf elderly people as so many of them spoke so loudly all the time. It would not have bothered most people and was unintentional, but right now even slight amounts of noise cause her head to hurt terribly.

Functioning normally is impossible. Frank is shivering in the bed with high fevers; and I cannot drive, read small print, or even watch television. Some of the time light is so painful that I walk through the house with a blindfold; and, at night, I make sure all the lights are out before I walk into a room. I cannot even get to a doctor if I want to go, which I do not. After the one day of improvement in the hospital, Lisa relapses back to the same intense pain as before. As if all this is not enough, Lisa's arm is burning and causing her even more discomfort. We surmise that the penicillin which is very irritating to the vein is causing problems perhaps because it is in the wrong vein. The cassette pump at home is delivering the medicine in much more concentrated doses than in the hospital probably resulting in the problem surfacing when we returned home. After two days, we discontinue the medicine; the pain is just too much to bear.

We are in a fine fix. Neither one of us is physically able to lift and transport her to have another PIC line inserted.

Noel Botsch from Option Care is very sympathetic to our plight and somehow makes all the arrangements to have a new line inserted. The nurse who does the procedure notices that my pupils are unequal. This scares me, and I know that despite my reluctance I will be forced to seek professional help. At least, the doctor will be able to see that something is obviously wrong--I think.

Despite my reluctance to ask for help, we are now forced to do so. Our neighbor comes to stay with Lisa so that Frank can take me to the doctor. If someone deserved a "Neighbor of the Year" award, our neighbors do. They have looked after our place while we were in the hospital and fed the dog. They have been increasingly concerned about Lisa and tried to help her through the pain and boredom by bringing over videos and flowers. In typical Lisa Marie fashion, she has found her way into their hearts. They love her. Lest you think that this is motherly exaggeration, they have talked of taking her on vacation in Europe with them. When a couple close to sixty wants to bring along an unrelated teenager, they must think quite highly of her.

The ophthalmologist listens to my story about the Lyme disease in our family and candidly admits that he knows nothing about Lyme disease. After all, it is not supposed to be in this area. He does find that I have iritis, inflammation of the iris. My pupils are unequal because they have become fixed from all the scar tissue that has formed. The cause is unknown and the treatment is steroids to reduce the inflammation and dilating drops to try and break the pupil free of the scar tissue. My vision may or may not return to normal. It could go away in a month or last the rest of my life. Curiously, it seems somehow to be related to arthritis.

After the ophthalmologist tells me that my vision may not return to normal, Frank becomes very upset with me for waiting a week to go to the doctor. He had often said that he believed that I would rather die than go to the doctor. I mostly considered doctors someone to go to when you had a baby. After Jonathan was born, I managed to avoid them for five years. But--I do not want to go blind.

THE HOSPITAL AGAIN

Convinced that this somehow relates to my other symptoms of nausea, fatigue, and joint pain, I call Dr. Masters with the ophthalmologist's report. Lyme disease <u>can</u> cause iritis and many other eye diseases. After considering this new manifestation in conjunction with my other complaints, he puts me on oral antibiotics. Four of five family members are now being treated for Lyme.

Two torturous weeks follow. Lisa seems to still be slipping. Though we try to be optimistic, the evidence of our own eyes prevents it. We have for the most part discouraged visitors; she is just in too much pain. A few people have come over, and they are shocked at the change in Lisa. They ask questions like, "How do you stand it?" and "Why isn't she in the hospital?" Cards, letters, phone calls, flowers, and packages are beginning to arrive from at least nine states. Each day the one thing that brings the most joy and excitement to her day is the mail. Somehow these cards and letters are tangible evidences of the love of her friends and family. They are her link with the world before Lyme.

Our friends and relatives are stunned by what is happening to Lisa. The fact that it is a mostly unknown communicable disease makes the whole story even more astounding. Even the people who have heard of the disease do not have any idea of how serious the repercussions can be. These people think of the Lisa they last saw; happy, vibrant, and extremely active. They cannot seem to reconcile the memory with the facts we are now giving them. Lisa always has had a Pollyanna-ish spirit; quite simply everyone loves her. Across the length and breadth of our nation, prayers are going up for our much loved little girl.

Pain has an Element of
Blank--
It cannot recollect
When it begun--or if there
were
A time when it was not--

Emily Dickenson

That the trial of your faith
being much more precious than of
Gold that perisheth,
though it be tried with fire,
might be found unto
Praise and Honour and Glory
at the appearing of Jesus Christ.

I Peter 1:7

CHAPTER EIGHT

What Next?

Wearily, we pack our bags to return to the hospital. We have only been home two weeks. Tests are to be performed to rule out the presence of any other cause for her illness. Her headache is so severe that now, like David at his worst, she will no longer watch television or read. The pain medicines do not seem to help very much. The days pass very slowly, but to count our blessings, she is still sleeping at night.

An MRI reveals nothing but abnormal sinuses for which she has familial tendencies. She is still eating very little, but with coaxing she does eat. We remind her that one eats to live not for pleasure. Within a few days of returning to the hospital, her headache progresses to the point that she does not want to lift it even to sit up and with our help use the bedside toilet. Each downward progression is humiliating to our modest, little daughter. Before her illness, she would have double-bolted the door to the bathroom if she could. Now her pride is reduced to submitting to bed baths and bedpans. She hates it fiercely.

After a few days we are transferred to Pediatrics. When we were admitted, there were no private rooms available in Pediatrics so we had opted for another floor. A private room was an absolute necessity with her insistence that there be no noise and very little light. Except for her severe joint pain and lack of chest pains, she now is behaving exactly as David did. The description of the headache is uncannily familiar. David called the pain nails; she calls it knives. A neurologist is called in for his opinion.

The neurologist orders EEG's, other nerve tests, and a spinal tap. All these tests come back basically normal. The elusive Lyme spirochete is winning again. I can almost hear a taunting sing-song voice chanting, "Ha, Ha, Ha,

Ha. You can't catch me!" However, within a couple of days of the headache so bad that she will not lift her head, the sedimentation rate is elevated. Again we are horribly familiar with this routine. Two children, with widely divergent personalities, have reacted with precisely the same mystifying refusal to lift their head in the presence of this headache.

The nurses on Pediatrics have never seen anyone in Lisa's condition. Most of them do not believe her. It is as simple as that. One nurse tells me, "No one knows how bad her headache really is." I reply, "Yes that is true. No one knows how bad her headache is, but when you make a statement like that it implies that you do not believe that it is as bad as she says that it is." I try vainly to explain the situation and how sick her brother was. Nothing is going to work. I have been through this before; the opinion is formed. The pressure from the nurses increases. Their opinion is that she is depressed and that they can somehow lift this depression. Finally, I tell Lisa to at least talk and smile some with these people or they are going to put her on antidepressants. She makes a supreme effort at my insistence. This only increases their suspicions that she is not really in pain. One morning a nurse asks her how she is feeling. Honestly, she whispers, "Terrible." The nurse chides her, "Terrible! I think you just have a bad attitude." Lisa cries. Not being believed by a nurse is a cruel blow to a child who has always striven for approval especially from authority figures.

The nurse continues with her amateur psychology, telling Lisa that when she is ready to get up and walk there is a cute boy down the hall. I bite my tongue hard. This is insane. Though to this nurse in her twenties this may be the ultimate motivation to my twelve-year-old daughter, boys are still something to be giggled over with a girlfriend. She does not actively pursue them. A girl her age would actually be of more interest at this stage in her life. Notwithstanding, there are an abundance of both sexes at home. Knowing my daughter quite well, I am aware of the biggest carrot the hospital has to offer--the newborn nursery. This has been discussed by the two of us; and she anticipates visiting there as soon as she is some better.

Hospitals have been forever banished from their former position in my mind. No longer are they great, hulking citadels warding off pain and death which I pass while making a mental note of the location just in case I have need of them while at the same time thanking God that I am not within their walls. Instead they seem to have transformed into gigantic, groaning machines with me but a small, mismatched cog in the internal workings; and yet the wheels keep turning, grinding, forcing me to conform or be consumed.

Being in the hospital creates pressures that we had not imagined. You expect to be concerned about your loved one and just by the very nature of the sleeping facilities, extremely tired; but what is totally unexpected is the loss of control. Frank and I have always tried to willingly submit to God, to each other, and to the laws of our country; but when it comes to abdicating our parental rights, we are not prepared to do so. We bring our child to the hospital for the staff's expertise in treating a medical problem, and yet each treatment, procedure, or drug must pass our scrutiny and approval because of our great love for and intimate knowledge of this particular child. We consider ourselves an integral and important part of the medical team believing God has placed her in our care and under our supervision. Not all parents are brainless idiots functioning totally at the mercy of their emotions, but perhaps because of a few this is the way oftentimes we are treated.

Thoughtfully, I consider my children. Though I know I am their mother, I have always believed that they compared favorably with other children in many areas. They are kind, considerate, and obedient. They have been taught how to work. Lisa mowed the yard all last summer, in addition to her household chores. David washed cars in the neighborhood, earning twenty-two dollars in one day. In all their athletic endeavors, they have pushed themselves to excel. They have never been thought of as crybabies, and I do not remember either of them ever crying after an injury on the field or in the gym. Though we have not had any serious medical problems, they have never seemed to exhibit any strange inability to deal with the occasional earache, stomach virus, or sore throat. In fact, when Lisa was two, her ear drum burst without her displaying any crying or discomfort. The pediatrician was terribly irate that I had not brought her in sooner and did not believe me when I said that she had not exhibited any pain. (It seems that "good " parents do not exist, you are either overly concerned or negligent.) She has had eight primary teeth and four permanent ones pulled to prepare for her braces. When the first ones were pulled at the age of four, the pediatric dentist wanted to give her laughing gas to make her relax as was his standard practice. I refused saying she would be fine, and not being the slightest bit afraid, she had nary a problem. When she had the allergic reaction to Ceclor at age four and a half, her feet swelled to twice their normal size and she was covered with a rash. Her feet were itching so badly that she spent the entire night sitting on the bathroom vanity her feet in a sinkful of cold water reading books. Periodically, I would get out of bed, bring her another armload of books, and encourage her to come to bed, but she would refuse. How many four-year-olds could sit up all night alone and entertain themselves while they were sick? Sometimes when I remember what a mature little creature she was, I marvel, especially since I have had the boys. Do my kids really not possess the courage, stamina, fortitude, or sheer willpower to withstand this headache? Could other children handle this same headache with greater fortitude? I have serious doubts that they could; but then I do not know this for sure, nor can I prove it. I make a decision. If, in fact, they do not have as high a pain tolerance as other children, it is not important to me. They are great kids. I am proud of them. I am convinced that they are fighting this to the best of their ability. That is all anyone could ask of them.

Lord, I am so terribly tired and emotionally exhausted. I do not want to lose my temper with these people, but I am terribly afraid that I am going to do so. I know that they are acting out of ignorance, but it would be ever so much easier if they were not hurting my daughter. I can take the criticism so much better than she, and she is already hurting so much. This is the little baby whose fingers and toes I counted, whose downy head nestled at my breast. Oh, she does not look like a baby anymore, but to us that part of her will always be inseparably intertwined with the person she has become. We seem to be getting a lot of practice at forgiving lately. Somehow I do not feel like I am getting any better at it. Please, help me to deal with this, Lord.

Another symptom begins to insidiously make itself known. Her skin is sensitive in various places. She does not want us to touch her anymore. The most cuddly child in the world does not want to be touched. The boys were not cuddlers. They were much too active to ever sit still for being

WHAT NEXT?

rocked, but Lisa was rocked for hours. What sort of symptom is this? I have never heard of this; and, obviously, the nurses and physical therapist have not either because they do not believe it for a minute. At least we can still kiss her face and hold her hands. These have been spared this bizarre manifestation.

A genetic test called HLA-DR4 typing has come back positive. From what we can understand this indicates a genetic predisposition to developing severe symptoms to Lyme especially the arthritic symptoms. I had been puzzling endlessly over why Lisa was flat on her back in the bed when others who have had Lyme for a longer period of time seem to be up and walking around. Dr. Masters says that he has seen other cases where the disease is truncated. Perhaps this genetic coding is the answer. In any case, I wish that I knew more. I wish that the doctors knew more.

The allergy scratch tests have proven beyond a shadow of a doubt that she is, in fact, allergic to the cephalosporins and Primaxin. We are running into a brick wall as to what to do. Dr. Masters has been so supportive through all of this. His compliments of our family have led us to trust him a great deal. It is a balm to our wounded spirits. He works so hard. Oftentimes when he comes to the hospital, it is after eight or nine at night. He is also traveling a great deal trying to educate physicians in the intricacies of Lyme disease. We appreciate his efforts on our behalf so much. We truly feel that we are very fortunate to live only three hours from his office. Without Dr. Masters we would have two extremely ill children instead of one and probably no diagnosis for either of them.

Dr. Masters wants to send Lisa back East to a pediatric neurologist who has treated a large number of Lyme cases. There we can have her desensitized to Claforan and be in the hands of someone who has treated some of the worst Lyme cases in the world. We decide to go. Uncharacteristically for Lyme, Lisa's decline has just been so rapid.

All Through the Night

Sleep, my babe, lie still and slumber,
All through the night
Guardian angels God will give you,
All through the night,

Soft the drowsy hours are creeping
Hill and vale in slumber sleeping,
Mother dear her watch is keeping,
All through the night,

God is here, thou'lt not be lonely,
All through the night;
'Tis not I who guards thee only,
All through the night;

Night's dark shades will soon be over,
Still my watchful care shall hover,
God with me His watch is keeping,
All through the night.

--Author Unknown

He will not suffer thy foot to be moved: he that keepeth thee will not slumber. Behold, he that keepeth Israel shall neither slumber nor sleep.
Psalm 121:3-4

CHAPTER NINE

The Hospital Saga Continues

Winging our way across a brilliantly blue sky sprinkled with fluffy, white mounds of clouds, the world outside looks so beautiful and normal looking. But our reality consists of a pitifully whimpering child lying on a stretcher. She has not walked in two and a half months, and it has been over two weeks since she has lifted her head from the pillow for any reason. Actually, there is no pillow. When her headache progressed to this amazingly agonizing severity two weeks ago, she pulled it out and has refused one ever since. She cannot bear even that slight amount of elevation of her head. Life's pleasures have been reduced to virtually nil. Eating brings no pleasure; the smell of food is nauseating. Music has always been one of her supreme joys; every night she would play her cassettes to drift off to sleep. Now music brings no joy only unremitting pain. Her vision is blurred and almost any light at all causes pain. Even a simple comforting touch is painful and unrewarding. Each day looms with the prospect of nothing but long hours of tedium and suffering. Our child still exists in this pain-racked shell, but she is almost unrecognizable.

Federal Express has been really good to us. Though our insurance does not specifically cover an air ambulance, they have arranged for one. Their policy of caring for their employees is certainly well deserved in this instance. The boys have been shipped to Ohio to stay with Frank's parents. At least, they will be spared the boredom and difficulty of trying to remain still and quiet in the hospital and motel. And we will be spared the difficulty of trying to make them.

The arduous journey is completed and we are settled in a beautiful, brand-spanking new room. Lisa is interested only in some pain medication. After a history is taken, the medication is finally administered; and she mercifully falls asleep.

The pediatric neurologist we are seeing is a most dedicated and unusual doctor. She truly cares about her patients, coming to the hospital every day of the year including holidays and treating the most difficult patients, the ones no one else will touch with a ten foot pole. It is no easy job. There are so many unknown aspects to Lyme disease, and the fight must take place with primitive weapons and unrevealing tests. I hope that one day she and Dr. Masters will both receive the accolades from their colleagues that they so richly deserve.

Finally, the nurses who surround us are familiar with Lyme disease. Eagerly, I ask questions, "Have you seen skin sensitivity before?" Having seen the condition often, the nurses are not surprised by it. It is a neurological manifestation; so that explains it. In response to my inquiry about other Lyme patients, they assure me that there are several Lyme patients here. I desperately want to talk to someone who is going through this same experience. Are there really other people suffering these agonies? How long did it take them to recover? As time goes by, we discover how abysmally ignorant we are and how naively optimistic are our expectations.

One of the sweetest nurses wants to put an egg crate foam pad on the bed to make it more comfortable. I decide against explaining the extent of Lisa's pain, pull her from the bed, and hold her sitting up in a chair. I do not cry. In fact, I cannot at this moment feel anything. The nurses are shocked at her response. They take one look at the tears streaming down her cheeks and her agonized expression of pain and swiftly make the bed. Giving her a pain shot, they cancel physical therapy and no one mentions making her sit up for a long while. Finally our caretakers are sympathetic to our predicament, and in some ways that eases the stress and pain of the situation.

Crraack!! In this most modern of hospitals, the doors have an electromagnetic field which allows them to shut automatically in the event of a fire but which, in breaking the field manually to shut the door, also causes a horrendous noise. They are not really made to remain shut, but Lisa's noise sensitivity is so severe that she cannot stand all the hustle and bustle that transpires in the hall. However, just closing the door causes a tremendous amount of suffering. Slight noises that normally do not even reach your consciousness bother her immensely. Thoughtlessly, I will crumple a paper and then feel awful at her moan. No matter how carefully I sink into a chair, it will creak slightly or the pillow will "whoosh" with escaping air. These, to me, minuscule noises take on gigantic proportions when magnified through her ears. We have requested that no one call us in her room because her reaction to the phone ringing is so intense. If someone calls who she thinks should know better, she is very upset for she feels that they do not care. Pitifully, she will ask, "Did you tell them that I have a headache, Mom?"

The Ronald McDonald House sends over the fluffiest, floppiest dog imaginable which she promptly christens "Cuddles." Frank just as promptly nicknames her "Puddles" and is rewarded with an almost smile and a quiet admonition, "You won't call her that when the nurses are in here. Will you, Dad?" Lisa and Cuddles will become inseparable.

The allergist who performs the desensitization arrives the first day. This is a long, fairly risky procedure. Despite the arrival of all the resuscitation equipment, the fears and risks are overshadowed by our realization of the magnitude of her decline. The sedimentation rate has elevated even more, and, just before we left Missouri, there was some loss of bladder control. We are traveling an unfamiliar journey with this most unfamiliar disease. We have no idea where the next twisting and turning could lead. We do know that recently an eleven-year-old girl has died from this disease. How did she die? We wonder just what finally kills you with this treacherous illness.

The desensitization takes even longer than was predicted as Lisa begins reacting to the second shot. In the last few months, she has undergone a spinal tap, an MRI, EEG's, nerve tests, and countless blood tests. Though these were incredibly painful in her present condition, none of these have produced more than a minimal amount of concern. But, this is different for all her life she has been warned that taking this particular medication could kill her. The fear sweeps her along like flood waters in a storm. We pile up sand bags trying to keep the swirling waters contained. We tell jokes, pat her hand, and fill cups with juice hoping to reassure her and take her mind off the procedure. At the same time, we have the unique opportunity to talk at length to a doctor and gain more information about the disease. He is most personable and has a son with Lyme making him sympathetic to our plight. After our experiences trying to find treatment for David, we are most extraordinarily grateful to anyone who helps us. Having the precious Claforan pouring into her veins gives us our first unadulterated hope in weeks. Today is Monday; we begin counting the days. Talking to others in the hall, we begin assimilating various pieces of information. One migraine sufferer reveals that the Lyme headache is a hundred times as bad as the migraines ever were. Just judging from our children's behavior, we had known this, but this confirmation from others is reassuring. Articles written by doctors and addresses of various Lyme publications become as precious as gold. After relating the problem of diagnosing David, one doctor tells us that the European doctors tend to look down on the American doctors for not recognizing the neurological symptoms of Lyme along with the arthritic symptoms. At least in our area there is the excuse of Lyme not being prevalent. The diagnostic horror stories we hear of these people who live on the East coast where this disease is rampant are incredible. This disease is so complicated that I can sympathize with the doctors, but surely when person after person has many of the same incredible symptoms, a pattern should begin to form. Surely if they read their literature, they can see the problems with the testing and that the rash is not always present. If they or a member of their family began exhibiting neurological symptoms and the CAT scans, MRI's, and normal exams showed nothing conclusive, would they consider Lyme and would they dispense antibiotics? I imagine so. So, why are the rest of us who do not have a doctor in the family reduced to defending our sanity and begging for the closely guarded antibiotics. Has medicine really reached such a pinnacle that the tests can completely rule out all physical ailments? Though I am very thankful for EEG's and MRI's, they have their limitations. One experiment with an EEG and a mannequin filled with green jello revealed a reading of life. And if you really pinpoint the doctors, they will admit that not all brain waves show on standard EEG's especially the deeper ones, and one-third of normal, healthy people's EEG's show abnormalities. I cannot explain why some of the common Lyme neurological symptoms do not manifest on these tests. Perhaps there is a chemical interference created by the spirochete or brainwaves yet to be discovered are the culprit, but, at any rate, the patient should not be blamed for the tests' inadequacies. One would think that the more one learns about the intricacies and complexities of our bodies, the more awe-inspiring they would become causing one to realize how much more there is yet to learn. If doctors were forced to work in the comparative darkness of the knowledge and tests of twenty years ago, there would be many diseases that they could not treat or understand which they can today. Likewise, twenty years from today, there undoubtedly will be advances that are earthshaking and completely unexpected. I believe that the knowledge which eventually will be gleaned from Lyme disease will produce many new and hitherto unimagined discoveries into the way our bodies work. If even a small percentage of diseases such as MS, ALS, Alzheimer's, lupus, chronic fatigue, and arthritis, diseases with no known cause or cure, are found to have the Lyme spirochete as the root cause, then it could revamp medical thinking in these areas. If one infectious agent can cause these problems, then perhaps there are others. As space research gave us many advances in medical knowledge and treatment, perhaps the sheer magnitude of problems associated with Lyme disease if thoroughly researched and unraveled could benefit many other disease victims.

Another problem seems to be in regards to length of treatment. We meet one twelve-year-old from New York who develops the rash and has a frankly positive test. Up to this time he has been a normal, happy child. After oral treatment, he is treated for three weeks on the IV antibiotics and told he should be well. He is not well. Now their pediatrician of seventeen years begins informing them that their child has psychological problems. Does this make sense? We have had ear infections treated with three different antibiotics with no response. Does that mean my child does not have an ear infection? And if this disease is in the central nervous system, the antibiotics now available seem to have a very difficult time penetrating the blood/brain barrier, making it much more resistant to treatment than a simple ear infection. I read in the newspaper that sometimes rheumatic fever, which is easily treated in the early stages with antibiotics, may once it has lodged in the heart, brain, and joints require life long antibiotic therapy. I wonder in my uneducated way if there could be some parallels with Lyme therapy. In the treatment controversy, many doctors are now climbing over the fence to the side of more aggressive treatment. As patients, we say, "Better to err on the side of too much treatment than too little." Most everyone who has had to deal with these problems is angry, and it is a very impotent anger. Though we cannot change our present situations, we all want to change the system so that it never happens again. After every conversation, we climb down off our soap boxes and wearily return to our own individual prisons constructed and maintained by millions of Lyme spirochetes.

More and more I find myself puzzling over the doctors' refusal to believe Lyme patients. Though not as common, I am sure that this problem of disbelief infringes in other areas of medicine as well. Some close friends of ours in another state have been fighting their own battle the past several months. When their thirteen-year-old begins complaining of problems with his vision, the doctor, unable to find anything wrong, tells them that he is lying. They do not believe this but do not convince the doctor although he does make an appointment with another doctor in another month. This doctor also can find nothing wrong except the optic nerve is a little white. He, too, sends them to yet another doctor in another month. The third doctor determines that the child has an inoperable brain tumor, an inoperable optic glioma. His future is uncertain. It is the largest tumor of this type that this particular large hospital has seen. Our friends feel badly about the two month delay wondering if they had pressed the doctors, if perhaps it would have changed the situation. Our own experience persuades us that this probably would have had little effect. How can doctors so easily and completely dismiss a patient's complaints as lies and hypochondria? Are we on trial? And are we guilty (lying or psychotic) until proven innocent?

One young resident says, "No one would doubt that your daughter has Lyme and is really in pain, but there are some children here who just want to get out of school." I already know that there are people who would doubt even someone in as severe pain as Lisa, but I am pleased to hear that at least this resident does not. I cannot imagine a child who would actually prefer hospital food and TV to the vast array of outside activities. I cannot personally vouch for any child but my own; though, with the ups and downs of his illness, I remember how easily David had been thought of in the same light as these other patients. Without proof, a patient is so helpless. By the time many of these kids are actually taken seriously (i.e. by the time the tests show incontrovertible, irrefutable proof of disease), there is irreversible brain damage. Sometimes I find myself wishing that I could give some of these kids' blood to the most adamant of the unbelievers. Are they sure enough of their position to take it? Would giving antibiotics to someone who they are not absolutely certain has Lyme compromise them so very much? I really believe that many aare afraid of being ridiculed if they were to make a mistake and call it Lyme when it was not. (When they are not afraid to remove an appendix or perform a hysterectomy without concrete proof, why are they so reluctant to merely dispense antibiotics?) Many doctors will say that they know about Lyme disease, when, in fact, they know very little. What I think that they actually mean is that they know enough to think that they do not need to know any more. After all, it is a rare disease confined to the Eastern seaboard, and the patient will have a large bull's eye rash to facilitate their diagnosis. Right? With a more accurate test, all this could change. Doctors would not have to be so uncomfortable making a clinical diagnosis and patients could be confident of the diagnosis. Would that there was more research to accomplish this dream for all of us. Would that no one else would have to suffer in the throes of undiagnosed Lyme disease.

Because Frank is in a fairly lucrative profession, we are coping financially though when we stop to add up the motel, restaurant, and telephone bills for the past two months we begin to feel a little sick. Suddenly, things like the ceiling on our insurance and our maximum deductible become important topics of conversation. We know that we are growing close to spending $100,000 of her insurance. This seems incredibly scary especially since we have met people who have used up all their insurance and sold their homes to continue treatment for their children. Some people had spent thousands of dollars just to get a diagnosis. And some are struggling with the travel expenses and staggering medical bills created by a high deductible. At least, at this point this is not an overpowering concern though it remains smoldering on a back burner.

On Thursday after three days on the Claforan, I awake to find my precious daughter sitting up in the bed. Quelling the wild hope that is racing through my mind, I tentatively ask how she is feeling. She seems to concentrate on her body trying to decide just what is different. Almost every symptom is better, the skin, the joints, the excruciating headache, the dizziness, the nausea, even the light and noise sensitivity. Everything is better, not gone but ever so much better. She wants to stand up. We feel like a miracle has just transpired before our eyes. She walks shakily wobbling like a newborn foal and with much support, but she WALKS. With eyes brimming with tears and voices choked with emotion, we call our families so that they too may rejoice. The medicine is working!

The next day she does not feel quite as well, but it is still such a vast improvement. We attribute the fatigue to overdoing to yesterday in our exhilaration and excitement. She still wants to practice walking though and our joy has not abated at this long awaited sight. Frank and I decide to go to lunch together and leave her alone for awhile. She is feeling better and is able to watch television so we are sure she will be all right. We are a little concerned about leaving because she is on the schedule for physical therapy. The ones in Missouri had not seemed to understand the disease at all, but we are told that the physical therapists here deal with a lot of Lyme and are very good.

When we return, Lisa is crying and looks terrible. We gather that physical therapy has been too much for her and chastise ourselves bitterly for leaving her. She has always been a submissive child, and she just did what she was told instead of firmly explaining that she was too tired. She then starts a steady decline. For a while we pretend that nothing has changed telling her that she is just tired when she complains. Within a few days, however, she is back to flat on her back in the bed basically the same as before. We find ourselves wondering, "If we had not left that day would she be in this condition?"

I find myself questioning the role of physical therapy when Lyme disease is so rampantly raging in control. After Frank was burned in Viet Nam, he spent excruciating hours forcing his arm to bend. He knew that if he did not do so that he would never regain the full use of his arm. The pain of physical therapy is certainly useful and rewarding in cases of burns, trauma, and stroke, where the damage is irreversible without it. But in these cases the actual damage is done and the cause of the damage is totally removed, no longer creating even further obstacles. Though progress may be slow, there is progress and you do not totally lose what you have worked for overnight. With Lyme disease you may be flat on you back one day and the next free from many of the symptoms that were plaguing you the day before. How do you motivate someone to push and hurt when any slight thing they may accomplish can be wiped out with a slight surge of the disease? And when with a decline in the disease, these tasks can be accomplished with much less pain. Lisa is convinced that she is going to be well any day now. Do I dispel this hope to persuade her to push herself harder?

We find ourselves on a wild, unending roller coaster ride. The roller coaster has no brakes and the ride is screaming out of control, too scary to be fun. Careening crazily, we want off, but it never, ever stops.

Easter. Spring. The very words are synonymous with new life, hope, happiness, and joy. We make jokes about this approaching holiday being a good day to rise up and walk, but we are not really joking. Could Spring really come to this cold, barren existence we are living?

On our past Easters, Lisa always had a frilly, new dress to wear to church. Somehow when you only have one girl, you go a little bit overboard on clothes. And being the first grandchild on both sides, she always had more than her fair share. Her first few birthdays and Easters, I would change her clothes two or three times to ensure that we had pictures in all her new outfits and to prevent any hurt feelings. She has two new dresses in the closet at home, but all that she has worn in the last three months are comfortable knits and pajamas. Who would have ever thought that we would still be in the hospital at Easter?

Carefully, I exert a steady pressure resisting the urge to yank. Her hair causes me to despair. It is always such a mass of tangles. Have you ever tried to comb someone's hair while they lie flat on their back? Or comb out tangles without moving their head? With great difficulty, I have managed to wash it on a hairboard that you slip under the patient's head and then drain the water into a wastebasket. We use great handfuls of conditioner; but, even so, lying on the bed hour after hour causes her hair to be a constant rat's nest. When she does not want me to comb it, I keep threatening to cut it; but I really do not have the heart because this and her long fingernails are the one indication that she still cares deeply about her appearance. She thinks that it has grown a lot longer since she has been sick, and she is anxious to get well and see how it looks. In the last couple of years, she has learned to use a curling iron and other hair styling paraphernalia sometimes spending an hour or more working on her hair. This was incredible to her dad after being raised in a family of boys. He would knock on the bathroom door and ask, "Are you still playing with your hair?" Haughtily indignant, she would reply, "I am not playing with my hair! I am fixing it!" This scene was replayed many times, and each time I would laugh at their antics until I almost cried.

On Easter morning, she does improve. She does not feel as well as the time before, but enough to enjoy her Easter candy. The Ronald McDonald House where we are staying has given her an Easter basket large enough for at least ten kids. Our emotions are so close to the surface that when Frank first sees the gigantic basket left outside our room, he cries. That someone has cared enough to go to all this trouble makes this a little easier. We share with the nurses and several other children on the floor.

This lumbering machine (the hospital) has its own idiosyncrasies which separate it from the others and which you must learn if you are to function in its midst. You wake, eat, shower, and sleep, (if you can amid the shrilling IV's and constant activity) according to its predetermined schedule and ponderous procedure. The IV's in this hospital are a little different, but it has not taken long to master the button to push to stop its piercing scream. This happens whenever Lisa bends her arm even to brush her teeth or eat. Some nurses object strenuously to your manipulation of this forbidden object. It is against hospital policy; and when they are around, you sit on your hands. The shower is in the hall with no lock on the door which means you break all records hurriedly pulling clothes onto your still damp body constantly watching the knob to reassure yourself that it is not moving. I try not to concern myself with the thought of germs from the other patients and parents. On the days that Lisa is improved enough, I take her down the hall for a bath. This is an incredibly difficult process. Somehow I maneuver the wheelchair and the IV machine with its alarm blaring into the barely adequate space of the bathroom. Without unhooking the IV, undressing her is a tricky business. Then I lift her into the tub trying not to hurt her too much in the process. Thankfully, I do not have a bad back and have not had any trouble lifting her day after day. We wrap her arm in a towel to prevent the IV from getting wet; and as quickly as possible, I shampoo her hair and help her wash. By this time she is always exhausted, and I still have the worst part to go--hauling her out of the tub without dropping her slippery body or pulling out the cumbersome IV. By the time we are finished, I am soaked; but at least she is clean and sweet-smelling for the moment.

Helping Lisa with meals, brushing her teeth, combing her hair, bringing the bedpan or assisting her to the bathroom occupy some of the day, but it still leaves many hours of--nothing. Most of the time, she has refused to watch television. So, hour after hour goes by in silent suffering. She is too ill for small talk or even for me to read to her quietly. And amazingly, even with all the medication she is receiving, she does not sleep. Some of the time, the room contains enough light for me to read to myself. I have always been able to lose myself in a book, but here with my child unable to use the same escape, it is much harder to leave the room behind. Mostly, I sit in the dark, silent room praying and remembering.

On the rare occasion that I escape the dreary confines of the hospital, I find myself blinking in the sunlight and gulping greedy breaths of the crisp, slightly acrid air. I feel like Rip Van Winkle, as though I have been asleep for a hundred years. Scanning the scurrying, busy people and rumbling traffic, I realize that it is not their world that has changed, but mine. The nurses keep telling us of all the tourist spots and urging us to go before we leave. I smile and agree, "Oh yes, I'd love to see the Statue of Liberty." Maybe it is not really a lie. Because I would love to see it--just as soon as Lisa is well. Could anyone really enjoy seeing such a grand symbol of freedom when their daughter was being held prisoner and tortured by such a wretched disease?

Chatting with a nurse one day, I find myself using the term "Peds", the abbreviated nickname for Pediatrics used by the nurses. Stopping in mid-sentence, I find the nurse staring at me strangely. Embarrassed, I feel my face turning red and try to explain, "I said 'Peds'." Now she really looks at me strangely and says, "So?" Quickly murmuring that I do not use that term, I go on with what I was saying. I do not know how to explain that the use of that term indicates a familiarity with something that had seemed extremely foreign when I first arrived. That familiarity means that I am an old-timer and learning my way around a place I do not wish to know. The feeling is most discomfiting.

The Ronald McDonald House has been such a blessing. After staying in the confined spaces of hospital and motel rooms for the past month, the spacious, home-like atmosphere is a welcome oasis. Somehow coming to this spotlessly clean, inviting place helps me draw the strength to return and face the relentless horror of the pain. Some nights to be still is impossible and the silence is too full of my own fears. Those nights there is always someone around to talk to, someone who is in a ssimilarsituation and shares your frustrations and anxieties.

The roller coaster begins a downward dip; gathering speed, faster and faster it races.

Lisa is growing steadily worse; we are beginning to despair. The pain is so unmitigating that she can no longer sleep. We begin trying various narcotics. To our amazement none of them seem to work on this pain. The pain moves around and intensifies like an orchestrated symphony playing in her body. And one feels that the Devil himself is conducting a host of demons in a strident, horrendous cacophony. One resident, our favorite, really likes Lisa and does his very best to help her. Late one night when he really should have been home getting some much needed sleep, he sits at her bedside unable to believe that the pain meds he has given have not provided her with enough relief to go to sleep. He keeps adding medications and none of them help. Finally after trying at various times, codeine, morphine, Vistaril, and Demerol, we move on to one of the most powerful drugs, Dilaudid. The pill form does absolutely nothing. She might as well have swallowed a candy. The shot form does provide enough relief for her to go to sleep, but something strange begins happening. While she is sleeping, her right leg begins to jerk spasmodically. By morning without her being aware of the episode, it has disappeared. She is still in tremendous pain. The chest pains which have suddenly made their appearance for the first time cause her such pain in combination with the other symptoms that all other thought becomes impossible. There is only the pain.

Flesh of my flesh, bone of my bone, her pain hurts me so intensely. She is the child who is most like me. Our personalities are like two peas in a pod. I can predict her reactions with the same level of accuracy as I predict my own. Please, Lord, let me have the pain. Let me bear this endless suffering.

THE HOSPITAL SAGA CONTINUES

Dark, sinister, foreboding, the pain permeates every corner of the room. Sharp talons pierce our souls causing us to writhe in agony and cry out to God for respite. The formidable enemy towers over us, dwarfing us. Enfolding, crushing, suffocating, the shapeless form chokes our spirits and slashes us with endless, futile questions. Lisa gasps pathetically, "Does God still like me?" We answer with examples of people who suffered in the Bible--Job, Joseph, and Daniel. Struggling to build her faith as well as our own, we recount their struggles and sufferings which seemingly had no purpose or plan for long years at a time. An then we speak of our precious Saviour who died for us and more than any other knows our deepest pain. Though difficult to explain, this sustains us, and the darkness in the room seems to subside.

I talk to my mother every day. The pain in her voice and her anxious daily questions magnify my own pain and helplessness. Everyone's unfamiliarity with this disease necessitates many explanations. They cannot believe that she is not dying or close to it when she is in this condition. The strain and pressure are very great. Unwittingly, I begin snapping irritably at the ceaseless questions. Does no one understand that I have no answers?

My biggest fear is not that she might die. That possibility is totally incomprehensible. The thought that terrifies and haunts me is that she might live . . . live in this deep valley of pain, misery, agony, and despair for the rest of her life. This horrible limbo between life and death is our lot. Clinging tenaciously to life, death tugs relentlessly but pulls her no closer to the precipice. And the ensuing battle only racks her body with endless pain and suffering. My hope is fading.

Comments about the future become unbearably painful. Innocent remarks like, "Maybe she'll be better tomorrow," grate on my raw nerves. For so long now, I had awakened each day expecting her to be well, only to have my hopes dashed in the face of even more misery and symptoms or to have the slight improvement of the day before erased. Tomorrow looms like an enemy, not a friend; and unknown dangers and pain lurk there. I can only deal with today and its problems. No more. The verse, "Take therefore no thought for the morrow: for the morrow shall take thought for the things of itself. Sufficient unto the day is the evil thereof," begins to have real meaning and depth in our lives.

The nurses want to change the sheets. They were not changed yesterday and they feel obligated to do it today. Knowing how much pain Lisa is in, they encourage her to have another shot of the Dilaudid, so that she can take the edge off the pain while they move her around just enough to change the sheets. I appreciate their tender care so much. Dealing with this pain is so impossible. You can see in their eyes that they do not want to come into the room. I do not blame them. Neither do I.

Within minutes of taking the Dilaudid, Lisa begins the jerking with her right leg and also her arm. The medicine dulls the pain somewhat, but the hard jerking movements are aggravating the joint pain and the continuous activity is extremely fatiguing. She is totally exhausted; consumed by the pain. As the jerking becomes rapid tremoring, another medicine is prescribed to stop this. It does seem to help. The tremors are slowing; but the side effects are tremendous. She begins hallucinating and projectile vomiting. Two nurses are trying to clean up the sheets and her while she continues to vomit violently all over them. When we finally have the vomiting somewhat under control, we still have to deal with a child who is not in contact with reality. She fearfully demands that the stuffed animals be removed from her bed because they are pulling on her. She says that she is floating, and then wonders, "What has happened to this room? It looks different." Looking at me very strangely, she asks uncertainly, "Why are there two of you?" Then she cries, "What is wrong with me?" Blessedly, she finally falls asleep for hours. Nothing causes her to stir.

In the hall, we laugh about the humorous aspects of the situation. The nurses seem surprised that we can laugh about it. Sometimes I am surprised too. Though the situation seems so desperate, life goes on. Though inside we are hurting so intensely, outside we smile and laugh and talk pleasantries. Sometimes I look at the face staring back at me in the mirror and wonder that the pain inside does not show. It is so strange to know that no one can know the extent of our pain or Lisa's. The worst physical pain that I have experienced was labor pains. I try to imagine being in labor for days at a time. The image is horrifying. The pain exists.

I cannot change it. I cannot wish it away or will it away. As a parent, I am helpless in the face of this threat to my child's welfare and happiness. I must place her in God's hands for I can do nothing.

At midnight the nurses are concerned as she continues to sleep so deeply, and though we request that she not be disturbed for the scheduled blood pressure and temperature check, they feel compelled to do so. After she is awakened, she cannot fall asleep. At least, the tremors have vanished. Frank passes the night blowing soap bubbles. Anything to try to forget the pain. Finally, around four in the morning, he requests another shot of the Dilaudid thinking that maybe they both can get some sleep. Almost immediately, the tremors begin. Three times now the tremors have started after the Dilaudid was introduced into her system. Somewhat slowly we begin to make a connection. There is no pain relief with her body shaking so violently. We make a decision. No more narcotics. The price is just too high and the rewards seem minimal. As the Dilaudid wears off, the tremors gradually cease. She sleeps on and on and on. In her exhausted state, she sleeps for sixteen or seventeen hours, only awakening when the nurses check her blood pressure or temperature.

The roller coaster sluggishly starts its uphill climb.

The next morning she is again better. She is able to sit up and watch television. Walking is still very painful. We begin making plans to go home. We do not know how long this tenuous improvement will last. But all that can be done has been done. We need to retrieve our boys and return to the sheltering privacy of our home.

CHAPTER TEN

One Day at a Time

Returning home is filled with obstacles and fraught with difficulties. Each stage of our journey must be planned carefully as she cannot walk at all and just sitting up is extremely painful and tiring. We know that we will attract enough attention with her in this minimally improved condition. If she slips the slightest amount, we are not sure that they will even allow us on the plane. We choose a plane that is basically empty. This will enable her to lie down after takeoff, and hopefully we will not exhaust her so much that she relapses again. We are also hoping that we can avoid a bathroom visit on the plane. How will we manage that situation in a miniature, plane-sized bathroom? Frank carries her onto the plane attracting as many disbelieving, horrified stares as I had feared. With the PIC line, her obvious pain, and her complete disability, people are more than a little bit curious as to the nature of her illness. I am also concerned about the air sickness that she normally has even in her healthy state. Despite my concern, we are spared this particular affliction. She tolerates the ride to the airport and the flight fairly well. To everyone who asks we try to give educational explanations, warning them of the unsuspected dangers of ticks and the difficulties of diagnosing Lyme disease.

The first most difficult part of the journey is accomplished. We find a motel with a ground floor and eagerly look forward to reuniting with the boys. Frank leaves us resting and goes to pick them up at the airport. Jonathan and David are crushed when they find that Lisa is not there to greet them. Jonathan cries for in his mind if she was coming home, then she must be well. He is totally unprepared for the sight of her still lying in bed and in obvious pain. Somehow, going home in this condition is a blow to Lisa's spirits too for she had thought that she would be well when she came home also. But just being together is a joyful experience. We had missed each other dreadfully. After calling me Grandmother a couple of times, Jonathan remarks, "Well, I know you are Mom because you smell the same." Somehow I think this is a compliment.

On the way home we have scheduled doctor's appointments with Dr. Masters for the rest of us to ascertain where we are in regards to treatment. My eyes are better, but I am still using the cortisone drops to reduce the inflammation. David continues to do very well, except for the two to three days a month that he relapses. Frank is much better. His symptoms have almost disappeared. I am still concerned about Jonathan. Though he has not developed the full blown symptoms of the others, he does seem to have occasional joint pain, headaches, and temperatures. In fact, he complained of his knees hurting before Lisa did. He is the only family member not taking antibiotics, and the thought of facing this disease with another child is devastating.

We arrive home just a few days before Lisa's thirteenth birthday. She has looked forward to this birthday for a long time. Becoming a teenager is a very special milestone to adulthood. Mercifully, the Lord blesses her with a better than average day. She is able to come to the table and have the dinner that she chooses, pizza naturally. What else would you have for a teenage party? I had hoped to have a real party just like every other year, but it is obvious that she just is not up to a crowd. Her presents consist of craft projects, things that one can do sitting down. These are a far cry from the horse we had planned. We take videos of her PIC line and sing "Happy Birthday" very softly. And all the while my heart is breaking into tiny little pieces for what might have been.

Our lives have been inexplicably altered. The future veiled by dark clouds of uncertainty. Though we have tried to return the boys to as much of a normal life as possible, the illness has a detrimental effect on all of us. Periodically, Jonathan asks, "Is Lisa going to die?" or "Is she ever going to get well?" We field the questions as much as possible trying only to live one day at a time though my own questions plague me with an even greater frequency and intensity than his. "How long is this terrible pain going to last?" "Will she ever walk again?" "Will she ever be a normal teenager again?" "Will she ever get married?" "Be able to have children?" "Go to school?" "How long can I stand this?"

We have been home from the hospital for two months now. She has not walked in a month, but thankfully there have been only two days of the excruciating headache, when she is unable to lift her head off the pillow. With her so completely incapacitated, I feel uncomfortable leaving her alone for any length of time so I arrange for someone to come and stay with her several times a week as I transport the boys to baseball games and activities. Much of the time, I do not believe that she could get out of the house if there was a fire. It feels very strange after all these years to only put out four place settings for a family meal. Instead, we make a tray. She is unable to bathe alone. Every day her cassette pump must be changed and we dispense a dozen or so pills. A nurse comes to our house once a week to do blood work. Medical routines and jargon have become an integral part of our life.

I read and reread the literature trying to find some tiny clue that might help. I make phone calls back East trying to stay in contact with fellow sufferers who may stumble upon some small helpful tip. They all have their own horror story. Gradually, bit by bit I come to the realization that these people are not getting well. Lisa is not the only person who does not seem to be responding well to the antibiotics. Some people are better than others, but then they were not as bad as Lisa to begin with. Everyone does seem to improve some, but returning to their former selves seems an unreachable dream at this point in Lyme disease treatment. Everyone has quite a bit of hope. The disease is caused by a bacteria, not a virus like AIDS or cancer. Bacteria are susceptible to antibiotics. It should be a simple matter of finding an antibiotic that completely kills the organism in the human body. Also unlike some incurable diseases, the root cause of Lyme disease has been identified. On the down side, there is very little research being done. All Lyme research worldwide in a year's time would fund AIDS research for only eight hours. For a disease which according to the CDC is the second most rapidly emerging disease in the nation, after AIDS, this does not seem like enough. If you live in an area populated by ticks or at any time visit such areas then you to are at risk. Avoiding the ticks is not an easy maneuver especially with children who turn somersaults in the grass and get down on their knees to crawl through the bushes. Already despite the precaution of Permethrin (the best poison on the market) applications and regular tick checks, Jonathan has been bitten by two ticks this summer. One embedded inside his ear canal, a place we had not thought to check. We all agree that to keep our hope alive, there must be more research. And to prevent further outbreaks and misdiagnoses, there must be more education for the public and the medical profession alike. We keep hoping and praying for a miracle.

Concerned friends want me to be sure and get out enough. How do I explain that I cannot run away from this problem? Summertime is here and everywhere I go, I see carefree teenagers enjoying their freedom. Images assail me of a slim, tanned Lisa poised on the edge of a shimmering pool; of a grinning girl hair whipping behind her as she pumps her bike; of a strong, muscular leg delivering a well-placed blow that carries a soccer ball the length of the field; of lithe, limber limbs that perform cartwheels, aerials, and backflips with an effortless ease; of the piano echoing through the house with her favorite pieces; of a beautifully dressed and perfectly coifed young lady going out with her friends; and on and on and on. Going shopping reminds me of how much she used to love trying on new things. Buying groceries, I am constantly trying to find something new and different and yet nutritious to tempt her appetite. Cleaning her room brings me face to face with her trophy collection and brand-new roller skates, an untouched Christmas present. Going to church on Mother's Day, it does not dawn on me until I am there how incomplete and bereft I will feel with only two of my brood beside me. Outside, the barn is an empty, stark reminder of the horse she had desired so much and which we had intended to purchase for her birthday. The strong cords of love bind me firmly to her in ways that only a mother can understand. This bittersweet love so permeates every fiber of my being that the ache never leaves. Tears reside continually beneath the thin veneer that is displayed, and they are never allowed to escape their confines in the presence of others. Though sometimes in private when a phrase or picture hammers through the closely guarded barricades unexpectedly, they are released. Perhaps Erma Bombeck said it best, "The child you love the most is the one who needs you the most." When David was five, he put it this way, "Mom, you always love us, but when we are sick you **REALLY** love us!"

Lord, give me the strength, wisdom, and courage to be the mother that this little girl needs and so richly deserves.

We firmly believe that God has a purpose in all this. Without this confidence, we could not go on. Our lives are grounded on Romans 8:28, "And we know that all things work together for good to them that love God, to them who are the called, according to his purpose." Fervently, we pray for the healing of our daughter, for the wisdom of the doctors, and for a definitive cure. As the song says, "Many things about tomorrow I do not know or understand. But I know who holds tomorrow and I know who holds my hand."

Every day Lisa sweetly whispers, "You are the best Mommy in the whole world." And each time, my heart crumbles because I cannot ease the suffering of the sweetest little girl in the world. This aching knowledge "blooms in me like a rose filling my chest with thorns."

With its unwilling, unwitting passengers, the roller coaster careens dizzyingly on its way.

EPILOGUE
June, 1991

The roller coaster has stopped at the top of a hill, shuddering occasionally in the breeze. No rescue attempt seems imminent; but with the unaccustomed stillness, our hearts are slowing and our breathing is less labored. We do not look down the steep incline where we are perched so precariously at the top. It is enough for now just to be still.

Lisa is better, the best that she has been since the illness began in December. We acquired a new antibiotic which in combination with the Claforan has wrought a remarkable transformation from the girl lying in such pain in the bed. After five days on this new medicine for the first time in five months, she can walk upstairs, play the piano, go shopping (in a wheelchair), go to a junior high party, watch her brother's baseball games, go outside without sunglasses, listen to music above a whisper, and on and on. The headache is still there but much better. The joint pain is also still there but much better. When the distance is not far, she does not have to be in the wheelchair, which she despises. She has begun riding a stationary bicycle trying to rebuild her strength and is doing her stretching exercises trying to regain her flexibility. The remnants of her gymnastic training and her superb physical condition at the beginning of this illness enable her to make a dramatically speedy comeback. Within a week, she is walking normally without any trace of a limp. We watch the miracle with thankful hearts. Thankful for each small task that she can now accomplish. She can now fix her hair and has taken an interest in her appearance and clothes again. She is reaching out to her friends again; calling, writing letters, and visiting. One day she even bakes cookies and cleans up the kitchen. Life now holds more joy than sorrow; more happiness than pain.

Being only human parents, we still yearn for the whole child that we had before Lyme. At the mall, she excitedly positions her wheelchair to watch a troupe of gymnasts perform. A short time ago, she could do every intricate maneuver that these girls are executing. Tears roll down my cheeks as I stand behind her trying to persuade her that we should move on. She tells me to go ahead and spends an hour watching the performance. When I return, she is clutching an advertisement for the gymnastic club wondering if she can join when she is well. I say, "Of course."

The confines and limitations of this illness are too restrictive, forcing ill accepted defeats. When we try to make her lie down and rest in the afternoons, she resists saying, "I have been in bed enough." Missing camp and several other summer activities are big disappointments, but we remind her to be thankful for the sheer joy of the things she can now do. She knows, but being only a human child, she impatiently struggles to regain the full life that she once knew. Unless pressed, she rarely mentions the pain that still pulses inside her body. After the agonies she has suffered, it seems insignificant, something to be ignored if humanly possible.

Time now almost resumes its laser-like, twentieth century speed, as we struggle to return to our lifestyle before Lyme. Things are just not the same when you have a child whose health, though much improved, is still so very fragile. Still, the months still fly swiftly and we rejoice as the PIC line is removed at the end of the summer. That line was a source of constant pain, irritation, and frustration as we fought site infections, line blockages, leaks, and raw skin irritated by the tape and dressings. We hold our breath as the oral medication continues to maintain Lisa's precarious position. She grows no worse, and we slowly exhale as we progress through Christmas. We keep reminding ourselves how much better this Christmas is than last year. And as she sings in a Christmas pageant with other teenagers, our whole family sits in the audience and cries tears of joy. Music, of necessity, has replaced her much-loved athletics; and, as much as possible, she spends her time at the piano.

The boys stay very, very busy with their athletics. David rolls from soccer to basketball to baseball. His basketball team played in the city tournament, and he is playing on a competitive baseball team. He is vibrantly healthy 99% of the time. It is hard to believe how very sick he was just eighteen months ago and how quickly he can become ill when we try to remove the antibiotics.

EPILOGUE

Frank and I are doing well and are off the antibiotics. Amazingly, all our old age symptoms, the arthritic aches and pains that we had kidded each other about, have disappeared with treatment. I quit using the steroids in my eyes over a year ago and have had no problems. The antibiotics worked better and with fewer side effects.

People often ask me, "Aren't you worried about all of you taking so many antibiotics?" My reply is, "I do not want any of us to have to take antibiotics or anti-inflammatories or steroids or any other medication, BUT I worry much more about the anti-inflammatories that Lisa has taken daily for months now and the steroids that I had to place in my eyes. The anti-inflammatories are known to cause ulcers. It does not seem to be a matter of if but of when. Steroids are infamous for their side effects, and the drops that the ophthalmologist told me that I might have to use for the rest of my life can cause glaucoma and blindness. The antibiotics by comparison seem so much safer and, most important, more effective. My question is, 'Without antibiotics, how many of us would still be walking? Without antibiotics, how many of us would still be functioning normally? Without antibiotics, how many of us would be <u>dead</u>? Without antibiotics, how much more pain, misery, and suffering could we have endured?' I thank God for the antibiotics and that we are able to take them. No, I do not want to take antibiotics any more than a diabetic wants to take their daily insulin shot or a heart patient his heart medication, but if it means the difference between life and death or endless suffering for my family then I will crawl across broken glass and walk on coals of fire to obtain them."

Lyme disease requires a longer treatment time than many illnesses that we are familiar with because it has a very slow reproduction time (cell division) and periods of dormancy. Other illnesses that have slow doubling times are tuberculosis and leprosy. The standard treatment for T.B. is two to four drugs used from six months to two years. Alan MacDonald, M.D., has grown cultures of *Borrelia burgdorferi* after 10.5 months of incubation, implying an 18 day generation time (normal generation time of most bacteria is 20 minutes). Comparing a normal strep infection which has a doubling time of twenty minutes and is treated for two weeks to ensure complete eradication of the bacteria, a Lyme infection proportionately would have to be treated for almost 25 years. But, the important thing to remember is that an optimal length of therapy has not been determined. However, the gap has narrowed between the groups advocating short term therapy and those who have observed that longer treatment produces better results. And, the gap has narrowed because the short term courses are being lengthened. Dr. Masters say that he knows of no one who treats Lyme less aggressively today than they did two years ago. And most doctors who treat short term have many caveats about re-treatment of relapses. I wish that the doctors knew exactly how long to treat and that they could find an antibiotic that is more effective. Meanwhile, I would rather take my chances with the antibiotics than with untreated, invasive, life-destroying Lyme disease.

Though Lyme disease has robbed us physically of so much, it has also inadvertently strengthened us emotionally and spiritually. Our family has grown closer as the result of the outpouring of love to each other while each one was sick. Though I would not have thought it possible, we love each other more; and the children know without any doubt that we love them. Because we faced this as a unit, as a family, we know that whatever else should befall us that we can battle it together. When facing a crisis like this, many unimportant trivialities of life regain their proper perspective. Things like leaky roofs and the economy do not seem so terribly important. We have grown closer to God because we were forced to rely on Him and not on our own strength. As the song says, "If I'd never had a problem, I wouldn't know that He could solve them." And as one of my favorite verses says, "For I am persuaded, that neither death, nor life, nor angels, nor principalities, nor powers, nor things present, nor things to come, nor height, nor depth, nor any other creature *(not even a spirochete),* shall be able to separate us from the love of God, which is in Christ Jesus our Lord."

In January, Lisa receives a positive PCR (polymerase chain reaction) test from the Texas Department of Health. This test, unlike the other Lyme tests which measure an individual's antibody response, tests for the DNA of the spirochete; and a positive result indicates that Lisa still has an ongoing infection even after months of oral and IV antibiotic treatment. We wait anxiously for the FDA's release of the new oral antibiotic, Zithromax; and finally in March, after a year of waiting for our family, we

EPILOGUE

begin treatment. At this time, improvement has been slight, but we have not given up the fight.

Still at the top of the slope on the roller coaster, we know that the slightest movement could jar us loose and send us plummeting downward. Scanning the carefree crowd below, we wait and pray for yet another miracle.

FACTS ABOUT LYME DISEASE

Lyme disease is a systemic illness caused by a bacteria, a spiral shaped spirochete called Borrelia burgdorferi. It is named after Dr. Willy Burgdorfer who discovered the spirochete in 1981. The illness itself was identified in 1975 in Lyme, Connecticut hence the name Lyme disease. Interestingly, two mothers were the first to recognize that an extremely large number of people in their area were afflicted with similar ailments. Though only recently specifically recognized, the illness has been present in the United States and other countries for many years. Mice pelts from the 1800's have been found to carry the bacteria. The disease is transmitted mostly by ticks, and the kinds of ticks which transmit the disease are being newly identified. All ticks should be treated as infectious and avoided. If you will be in a tick infested area, you should use an insect repellant containing DEET and a poison containing Permethrin on your clothes. Tucking your pants into your socks and wearing long-sleeved, light colored clothing may help you spot the ticks before they reach your skin. At least every two hours, you should check for ticks. Unless a tick has imbedded, it cannot transmit the organism. Estimates for the time of transmission vary, especially with the size of the tick. Larger ticks have been found to transmit the disease in less than four hours. Ticks should be removed with tweezors grasping as near to the skin as possible. Try not to squeeze the body of the tick. The area and the tweezors should then be disinfected with alcohol. Do not use nail polish, kerosene, or a match to try to remove the tick. These will only cause the tick to spew more infectious material into your body. If the tick is dead, it should be saved in a container of alcohol. If it is alive, place it in a plastic ziplock bag with a cotton swab slightly dampened with water. Keep in the refrigerator. Contact your local health department or the Lyme Borreliosis Foundation (listed under Lyme Publications) for information regarding testing.

In my untutored opinion, many people across the country may in fact have

Lyme disease and not even know it. Despite more stringent reporting guidelines in 1990, 44 states reported a total of 7,995 cases. The guidelines for a reportable case of Lyme disease are: 1. A person with erythema migrans (the characteristic bull's eye rash measuring at least five centimeters); or 2. A person with at least one late manifestation and laboratory confirmation of infection. The CDC emphasizes that these guidelines are for "epidemiologic case definition intended for surveillance purposes only." Conservative estimates would place actual new cases for 1990 between 40,000 and 80,000. And 1991, has shown a 17% rise in certified cases over 1990--close to 10,000 new cases last year. The disease is very difficult to diagnose and is often mis-diagnosed as multiple sclerosis, ALS (Lou Gehrig's), arthritis, lupus, Alzheimer's, and other illnesses. Early symptoms *may* include a characteristic bull's eye rash. Only about 60 per cent of the victims have the rash and others fail to notice this important symptom.[1,2,3,4,5,6] The other early signs, flu-like symptoms, are very hard to connect to Lyme unless you specifically remember a tick bite in the past month and are very informed about Lyme disease.

Later symptoms may include:

Muscles/Bones: Pain in joints, tendons, muscles, and bones. Pain may move around. Arthritis, particularly of the knee. Backache and neckache are common. Erosive synovitis, Baker's Cyst, vague fibromyalgia type syndromes, Reiter's Syndrome.

Neurological: Severe migraine-like headaches, meningitis, dizziness, seizures, numbness, tingling, cranial nerve dysfunctions of CN7 (Bell's palsy), CN3, CN4, CN5, CN6, CN8, facial twitches, carpal tunnel, difficulty walking, uncontrolled jerking (chorea), skin sensitivity, difficulty concentrating, impaired learning ability, changes in sleep pattern, mood changes, short-term memory loss, encephalitis, inability to talk, TMJ type syndrome.

Eyes: Light sensitivity, iritis, conjunctivitis, blurred vision, double vision, neuritis, blepharitis, panophthalmitis, episcleritis, uveitis, floaters, keratitis, vasculitis, papilledema, optic neuritis, Horner's Syndrome, Argyll Robertson pupil, blindness.

Ears: Noise sensitivity, ear pain, buzzing, ringing, impaired hearing, deafness.

Heart: Heart palpitations, irregular heartbeat, myocarditis, myopericarditis, pancarditis, heart block (first degree, Wenckebach, or complete heart block).

Skin: Variety of rashes. May or may not look like bull's eye rash Uticaria (regional or generalized hives), malar rash (reddening of the cheeks), erythema nodosum (red patches), and small evanescent erythematous patches and circles. Borrelia lymphocytoma on earlobes or areola. Acrodermatitis chronica atrophicans (A.C.A.), other lesions suggestive of scleroderma, sarcoidosis, erythema nodosum, pityriasis rosasia and granuloma annulare.

Gastrointestinal: Nausea, vomiting, diarrhea, gastritis, Lyme colitis, anorexia.

Lymph: Swollen lymph nodes.

Respiratory: Non-exudative sore throat, non-productive cough, respiratory distress syndrome.

Liver: Hepatitis.

Renal and Urologic: Urinary infections, microscopic hematuria, proteinuria, urniary retention, orchitis, prostatitis type syndrome, urinary frequency, and dysuria.

Endocrine: Possible endocrinopathies such as thyroid dysfunction.

Other: Unexplained weight loss or gain, severe fatigue, unexplained fevers particulary in the evening, altered taste, swollen testicles and gynecological problems, sinusitis, pharyngitis, increased motion sickness.

Pregnancy: Miscarriages, stillbirths, birth defects.

Any combination of symptoms can occur. And as the disease is cyclic in nature, they may come and go in a confusing manner. Test results that may be termed red herrings but which, in fact, may be red flags are elevated sedimentation rate, elevated liver enzymes, elevated muscle enzymes, white spots on MRI's, elevated cholesterol and triglyceride levels. The actual Lyme tests are filled with inaccuracies and problems. They test only for antibody reaction to the disease. Some people are just poor antibody makers and others have had antibiotics at the beginning of the illness reducing the body's build up. Many people do not have a positive test for months and some never. Strain variations also may make testing even more problematic. <u>A negative test result does not mean that you do not have Lyme disease</u>.[7, 8, 9, 10, 11, 12] The gold standard for diagnosing Lyme disease is, of course, isolating the spirochete. This, however, is a skill that has not been perfected; and, even under the best conditions, the frequency of isolating the bacteria from acutely ill patients is less than 10%.[13, 14] The spirochete that causes syphilis has never been cultured, simply because the researchers do not have the skills to do it.

Treatment for early cases consists of oral antibiotics, amoxicillin, doxycycline, or minocycline. As the disease can go dormant, treatment should continue until several weeks after symptoms are resolved to ensure complete eradication. Antibiotics are not always effective even on early cases. Late stage cases probably will need intravenous drug treatment, usually Claforan, Rocephin, or penicillin, though the newly FDA approved Zithromax, an oral drug, may be helpful in avoiding this in some cases. The spirochete can penetrate any organ and finding an antibiotic that also will penetrate into all these areas is difficult.

If you believe that you may have Lyme disease, you should contact the Lyme Borreliosis Foundation, a nonprofit organization in Tolland, Connecticut (P.O. Box 462). The phone number is (203) 871-2900. They can refer you to a physician who is familiar with Lyme. They also have more information on the disease.

If you believe that this is as dangerous and insidious a disease as I, please join me in calling or writing your senators and representatives asking for funding for more research. Money that is being squandered on unnecessary items could be better put to use protecting the populace from an incapacitating, communicable disease. As surely as billions of ticks will be climbing their relentless, unerring way to the top of a swaying blade of grass tomorrow, children and adults will be bitten and infected with Lyme disease tomorrow. Let us all do our part to prevent this needless tragedy.

References:

1. Berger BW. Dermatologic Manifestations of Lyme Disease. Rev of Infc Dis. 1989; 11(Supple 6): S1475-81.

2. Malane MS, Grant-Kels JM, Feder HM, Luger SW. Diagnosis of Lyme Disease Based on Dermatologic Manifestations. Ann Intern Med. 1991; 114:490-498.

3. Steere AC. Lyme Disease. N Engl J Med. 1989; 321:586-95.

4. Lyme Disease - Connecticut. MMWR. 1988;37:1-3.

5. Stanek G, Flamm H, Groh V, et al. Epidemiology of *Borrelia* infections in Austria, Zentralbl Bakteriol Mikrobiol Hyg [A]. 1986;263:442-9.

6. Duffy J, Schoen RT, Sigal LH. 1991 update on Lyme disease. Patient Care. June 15, 1991; pp 24-46.

7. Duffy J, Mertz LE. Serologic testing for Lyme disease. Ann Intern Med. 1985;103:458.

8. Barbour AG. The diagnosis of Lyme disease: rewards and perils. Ann Intern Med. 1989; 110:501-502.

9. Hedberg CW, Osterholm MT, MacDonald KL, White KE. An interlaboratory study of antibody to Borrelia burgdorferi. Infect Dis. 1987;155:1325-1327.

10. Dattwyler RJ, Volkman DJ, Luft BJ, Halperin JJ, Thomas J, Golightly MG. Seronegative Lyme disease. N Engl J Med. 1988;319:1441446.

11. Mertz LE, Wobig GH, Duffy J, Katzmann JA. A comparison of test procedures for the detection of antibody to Borrelia burgdorferi. Ann NY Acad Sci. 1988;539:474-475.

12. Corpuz M, Hilton E, Lardis MP, Singer C, Zolan J. Problems in the use of serologic tests for the diagnosis of Lyme disease. Arch Intern Med. 1991;151:1837-1840.

13. Steer AC, Grodzicki RL. Kornblatt AN, et al. The spirochetal etiology of Lyme disease. N Engl J Med. 1983;308:733-740.

14. Nadelman RB, Pavia CS, Magnarelli LA, Wormser GP. Isolation of Borrelia burgodorferi from the blood of seven patients with Lyme disease. Am J Med. 1990;88:21-26.

SUGGESTIONS FOR BETTER HEALTH CARE

A study by Katherine Linder, MLS, RN, in the *Journal of the American Medical Association* indicates that "uncooperative patients" recover faster. To a doctor, "uncooperative" means asking many questions, being persistent, researching one's own medical records. Yet patients who are knowledgeable about their condition and participate in the decision-making process receive better care from their physicians.

The following are some suggestions that I have compiled out of our experiences:

1. Know yourself or your child, as the case may be. Know how you normally react to stressful situations. Do you eat more? less? sleep more? less? Is there really an abnormal amount of stress in your life? What can you do to eliminate it? When the stress is lessened or eliminated, do your health problems remain at bay? YOU are the only person in a position to answer these questions and to determine if the health problems are somehow related. Beware though for much media attention has been focused on this subject and many of us have been brainwashed into believing that everyone is sick because of this rather vague entity that is currently in vogue.

2. Do not sabotage yourself by adding comments to your symptoms such as, "Maybe this is all in my imagination, but . . . ." or "Well, yesterday, I was fighting with my daughter, and . . . ." or "This is probably not important, but I had this little, tiny smidgen of pain . . . ." If you do not feel that it is important, then the doctor probably will not take it seriously either. If it is important enough to mention, then it is important enough not to belittle. A new study on women and heart attacks has shown a big discrepancy in the way women and chest pains are treated and the way men are treated with the same exact complaints. The study concludes that part of the problem is the percep-

tion of the doctors that women do not have heart attacks. But some researchers also feel that women exacerbate this misconception by minimizing their complaints and excusing them away.

3. I know that you have heard this before, but write it down. Make a list of symptoms and of the questions you have <u>in order of their importance</u>. This will save time and ensure that nothing is omitted. Doctors are usually very busy, and a silence is often an indication that the business is completed.

4. Be assertive. A study by sociolinguist, Richard Frankel, reported that more than half of the patients were interrupted by their doctor within the first 18 seconds of starting to describe their ailments. Insist on discussing **all** your medical concerns.

5. Particularly if you are not feeling well, take along a tape recorder. Many times when one comes home from a doctor's visit, it is hard to remember what they said caused this particular ailment and how long or what remedy to try. Also, at times they use unfamiliar terminology which then leaves you uncertain as to what they actually did say. A tape recorder can give you a chance to completely and thoroughly understand what was said.

6. Buy a PDR, Physician's Desk Reference, and a medical dictionary. The PDR lists most medications, their manufacturers, their side effects, possible drug interactions, and a host of other things. It will not make you a doctor, but it will give you much valuable information that can ease your mind about a particular side effect when you find that this has happened to other people and is not all in your head. Also, if you do not understand why you are being given a particular medication, it can tell you for what condition this drug is most commonly prescribed. You will most likely need the medical dictionary to interpret the PDR and to read your reports (next suggestion).

7. Always obtain copies of your health records. Of course, it is always possible that they may be lost, but more important than that is the fact that you need to know what they say. You need to know if this doctor is really listening to you and taking you seriously. You need to

SUGGESTIONS FOR BETTER HEALTH CARE 95

know if he has misinterpreted anything that you have told him. You need to know if there are any test results that have not been passed on to you. This can be a real problem. One mother insisted that the doctors run a culture on her three-year-old daughter's spinal fluid after the 30 days of supposedly adequate treatment for Lyme. The results came back highly positive, but the doctors not believing that the Lyme was causing the problems told her that the test was negative. Three years later she reads her records and finds out the truth but in the intervening years her daughter has no antibiotics, does not speak, and is developmentally retarded. Obtaining your records is time-consuming and costs a dollar or more a page at times, but it is worth your time and effort.

8. If at all possible and you are very ill, have an advocate, someone who goes with you on office visits and stays with you while you are in the hospital. Hospitals are understaffed often; and, even under the best of circumstances, mistakes in dispensing medications, administering tests, and even in taking the wrong person to surgery have occurred. Someone who is not ill and who can speak on your behalf is an advantage. We had a medication mix-up while in the hospital with Lisa. Had I not been there and positively asserted that she had been given another medication and not the one that was written on the chart, she would have had two doses of one medication much too close together and completely missed the other. After my continued insistence that this was the case, they called the nurse from the last shift at home and she confirmed what I had said.

9. Be persistent. Don't give up. Try, try again. Medicine is far from perfect, and the proof of this is as close as your nearest hospital or cemetary. Relatively few people die of natural causes relating to old age. With a difficult medical problem, the first diagnosis is not necessarily the correct diagnosis; and a second, third, or even more consultations may be the best way to explore your options.

10. Doctors are not God and do not think of them as individuals who can read our minds, instinctively know what is wrong, and never make a mistake. There is no way that they could possibly remember everything that they were taught in med school; and, even if they could,

medical advancements spew forth such a plethora of new studies and research that no one doctor could possibly read and digest it <u>and</u> maintain a practice simultaneously.

11. Some questions are better left unanswered or avoided especially those regarding your sex life, marriage, or job unless you can reply in a totally positive manner. Always clarify these personal questions, "What exactly do you mean by that?" and then give detailed answers. One friend was asked, "Has your sex life changed?" Now she had been married twenty-five years. She answered, "Yes." The resident pats her on the shoulder and says, "We are going to find someone to help you with this." She was infuriated. She did not need help with her sex life. She needed help with her pain and inability to work. I think that one of the doctors' favorite expressions is, "I didn't say that." Turnabout is only fair play. Especially watch out for this question, "What do <u>you</u> think is wrong with you?" When a doctor asked this question to a friend of mine, she almost screamed in frustration, "That's why I came to you . . ." After that, he took her seriously.

12. Document every symptom that you can. In the case of rashes, take pictures. Facial palsies and uncoordinated gaits can be recorded with a video camera. Keep a diary of symptoms and anything that you think could have possibly triggered them, i.e., food, exercise, heat, exertion.

13. Read, read, read. The bigger libraries usually have a medical section that contains at least some of the more popular medical journals. A medical library, of course, will be the most complete. There is a yearly index by subject matter. Keep an open mind. The very fact that this topic is the subject of research indicates that they have not learned all there is to know and many times the researcher has a preconceived idea about the project in the first place.

14. If there is a support group in your area for your particular illness, explore the possibility of at least visiting or even joining. The advantages can be many from finding another doctor or latest treatment to finding ways of coping. Support groups will often have copies of the latest research findings and information about political action

that may be proposed. And sometimes seeing someone in even worse condition than you are can give you that little boost to take your mind off your own troubles long enough to make them seem a little smaller.

15. Pray. There is Someone who knows what is wrong with you and has all the answers. This may seem hard to believe when you are suffering; but, the truth of the matter is, we are **all** going to die one day and most of us are at some point in time going to suffer in one way or another. I personally do not believe that God causes suffering and pain. I believe that this is all the result of sin and the Devil. However, I do believe that nothing can touch us unless God allows it. If there is no God and no hereafter, then all the suffering is senseless and meaningless. But, if there is a God who knows our every need and who is directing our lives, if the universe is progressing on a course totally in His plan, and if everything that happens, good and bad, is part of that plan, then Life takes on a different perspective. And that which seems unbearable becomes bearable with Him at your side. Not easy, not fun, not even without questions, but somehow bearable. May you find peace in the midst of your storm. His name is JESUS.

LYME NEWSLETTERS

Lyme Disease Update, Mrs. Charlene Glover, Editor & Owner
Route 1, Box 33
Mill Shoals, IL 62862   Phone: (618) 382-5293

ticked-off tract, Laura Ames, Editor & Publisher
Ames to Please Publications
325 Fresno Street
Coalinga, CA 93210   Phone: (209) 935-0914

Midwest LymeAid
Midwest Lyme Disease Support Group
P.O. Box 3135, Independence, MO 64055

Lyme Lines
Building 31, Room 7A32
9000 Rockville Pike, Bethesda, MD 20892

Lymelight
Lyme Borreliosis Foundation
P.O. Box 462, Tolland, CT 06084-0462

The Lyme Times, Phyllis Mervine, Editor
Lyme Disease Resource Center
P.O. Box 1423, Ukiah, CA 95482

Lyme Treatment News, Richard Lynch, Editor
National Lyme Community Research Institute
17 Monroe Ave., Staten Island, NY 10301   Phone: (718) 273-3740

Lyme Disease 1991: Patient/Physician Perspectives from the U.S. & Canada , Lora Mermin, editor, is a compilation of some of these newsletters and is available from Lyme Disease Education Project, Inc., P.O. Box 55412, Madison, WI 53705, for $11.95, shipping inclusive.